Alina Zubkovych

DEALING WITH THE YUGOSLAV PAST

Exhibition Reflections in the Successor States

Alina Zubkovych

DEALING WITH THE YUGOSLAV PAST

Exhibition Reflections in the Successor States

ibidem-Verlag
Stuttgart

Bibliografische Information der Deutschen Nationalbibliothek
Die Deutsche Nationalbibliothek verzeichnet diese Publikation in der Deutschen Nationalbibliografie; detaillierte bibliografische Daten sind im Internet über http://dnb.d-nb.de abrufbar.

Bibliographic information published by the Deutsche Nationalbibliothek
Die Deutsche Nationalbibliothek lists this publication in the Deutsche Nationalbibliografie; detailed bibliographic data are available in the Internet at http://dnb.d-nb.de.

∞

Gedruckt auf alterungsbeständigem, säurefreien Papier
Printed on acid-free paper

ISBN-13: 978-3-8382-0943-2

Printed in the EU

CONTENTS

LIST OF PHOTOS AND TABLES

1 INTRODUCTION

In 2009, Tim Judah introduced the descriptive term "Yugosphere," as a result of his observations of the reemergence of economic, cultural, and political ties of ex-Yugoslav countries. The economic links, which were broken in the 1990s, are being restored, and the neighboring countries collaborate as satisfactory export and import partners with each of the former Yugoslav countries. Bosnia exports to Croatia (17.2 percent) and to Serbia (14 percent); the import from these two countries to Bosnia is mostly on the same level. Macedonia largely exports to Montenegro (28.3 percent) and to Serbia (23.5 percent); 30 percent of Montenegrin products go to Macedonia. More than 11 percent of Kosovo's trade is either with Serbia or Macedonia or comes through them. Slovenia is not excluded from this list and plays the role of an important investor in the Balkan region; for instance, it was the sixth largest investor in Serbia in the 2000–7 period. Similarly, in Kosovo, Telekom Slovenia is the largest cable TV network operator in the country (Judah 2009, 4). Supermarket chains from Croatia, Serbia, and Slovenia (Konzum, Delta, and Mercator, respectively) are opening outlets across the region; tourism promotions are inviting Serbs to spend their time in Croatia; former Yugoslav brands, such as Croatian Kras and Vegeta, the Slovene Alpsko and Gorenje, Montenegrin wines, and Macedonian fruits and vegetables have returned throughout the region (Judah 2009, 5).

Culturally, Judah notes, these countries are also connected through the local TV channels that are broadcast in the region, as well as pop music, music festivals, or common websites for downloading books, such as Knizevnost.org. Furthermore, cultural patterns are similar. Thus, "anyone on Facebook with friends in the region can see people from one end of the Yugosphere to the other selling or looking for tickets for big bands playing anywhere from Ljubljana to Skopje" (Judah 2009, 9). Therefore, the given term is oriented toward the present to encompass the economic, political, and cultural connections that have appeared since the dissolution of the Yugoslav federation and can be described as "the social networks based on past and present connections of the Yugoslav and post-Yugoslav space" (Bieber 2014, 5).

Continuing Judah's observation, we may mention the similar intentions with which the given countries are represented toward the integration into the European Union (EU) space, if already not a part of it. Thus, Slovenia has been part of the EU since 2004, Croatia entered the EU in 2014, Serbia and Montenegro are candidate countries, Bosnia and Macedonia are cooperating within the frameworks of EU projects, and Kosovo is fully involved in the EU functioning by being patronized by international institutions.

Consequently, being connected economically and culturally, having common political strategies for entering the EU, can it be presumed that the ex-Yugoslav countries would have produced the similar national memory politics toward the pre-conflict period, that is, socialist Yugoslavia?

The assumption about the harmonized interpretation of the common recent past becomes more debatable if we take into account the ethnic conflicts that still arise. Thus, in September and October 2014 alone, different protests took place throughout the region. For instance, Montenegrin Serbs demanded an end to discrimination and "to protect the Serbian language and the Cyrillic alphabet"[1] in Montenegro; Belgrade both held the lesbian, gay, bisexual, and transgender (LGBT) pride event in September[2] and invited Vladimir Putin as the most prominent guest for the 70th anniversary of the liberation of Belgrade during World War II.[3] The celebrations took place for the first time since 1985 and were moved four days in advance so that the Russian president could be present at the event.

In the same year, the Yugoslavia War Crimes Tribunal in The Hague took place. In fact, there has been insufficient evidence to convict Radovan

1 Montenegrin Serbs Allege Language Discrimination, BalkanInsight, October 20, 2014, http://www.balkaninsight.com/en/article/montenegrin-serbs-call-for-language-discrimination-to-stop

2 Serbia Gay Pride march returns after four years, BBC News, September 28, 2014, http://www.bbc.com/news/world-europe-29399404

3 Putin guest of honor at Serbia military parade, BBC News, October 16, 2014, http://www.bbc.com/news/world-europe-29641642

Karadzic of the Srebrenica genocide.[4] Taking such a broad collection of facts into account, may we predict seeing differently constructed national narratives rather than harmonized interpretations? If so, how will the past be interpreted today in the successor states?

In my research, I would like to compare the representation of the Yugoslav period as it has been constructed by national historical museums of the former Yugoslav countries. I would examine history museums, which are located in the capital cities. Additionally, museums or exhibitions that are specializing in the researched period, located in the same cities, would be also taken into consideration. The selection criteria could be presented through three main categories of institutions, which we may choose for our research: history museum, museums of Yugoslav history, and temporary exhibitions dedicated to Yugoslav history. The third category, describing expositions either grounded on a private initiative or made in nonhistorical museums, may be added if its topic specifically deals with the representations of Yugoslavia. I use the capital's history museums in order to establish representativeness and to be able to compare all materials under the same conditions. Such sampling criteria enable perceiving the general trends in the construction of the national or official interpretations. However, it has to be mentioned that by focusing on a single type of institutions, we reduce possible multilayered narratives, presented in other cities, and in other types of public cultural spaces. This might be the case for Bosnia and Herzegovina or Kosovo, where several ethno-narratives are competing with each other on the same state level. Visits to Banja Luka, Mitrovica, or Vojvodina might have enriched the knowledge of the competing historical narratives; however, such research requires another design and sampling criteria. Therefore, we reduce our analysis to proposed sampling criteria and study only the main national museums.

My decision to use museums as the main object of analysis is grounded in an understanding of the given institution as a deeply political one, which functions not only for displaying the material and preserving items chosen

[4] Showdown at Balkan war crimes tribunal, Aljazeera, October 9, 2014, http://www.aljazeera.com/indepth/features/2014/10/showdown-at-balkan-war-crimes-tribunal-2014108161318449260.html

as heritage objects but also function as the space that helps different groups to use it in their interests and to compete with others. Therefore, the museum is understood by me as a place of the concurrences of the power and meanings; the place where the material talks not only about the history but also about the actors involved in creating meanings.

When I started my research, I determined the complex constructions of the recent past at the museums. The Yugoslav period was sometimes obscured in the museums but turned out to be alive at the pub right around the corner near the museum in one place, while being a "hot topic" in another museum. Sometimes, the museum was becoming a core place for demonstrations of public discontent and, through the activity of protesters, it was becoming clear that society is still actively discussing or labeling the given period in contrasting ways.

The events dedicated to topics somehow related to the issue of Yugoslavia were being and continued to be actualized through the museum space. If there was an opening of an exhibition dedicated to the political prisoners, it escalated the political activism and confrontation of different civil divisions that have a dichotomous vision of the recent socialist past. Such a case took place in Belgrade during the opening of the exposition in the History Museum in April 2014.[5]

Three months earlier in Belgrade, there was a massively promoted exhibition called "Good Life in Yugoslavia," which was inviting visitors to immerse themselves into the world of "unity and brotherhood." There, visitors were able to taste and even to smell Yugoslavia. A similar exhibition, but with the accent on the sacral role and personality of Josip Broz Tito, was gaining momentum in Ljubljana.

The characteristic of all of the aforementioned events was the unfailing popularity of pro- or contra-Yugoslav exhibitions. The aforementioned examples were merely the case of perceptional plurality and polydiscursivity for the broader spectrum of relations toward the past.

---

5 O politični represiji v Srbiji po drugi svetovni vojni (About political repression in Serbia after WWII), RTV 4, April 18, 2014, http://4d.rtvslo.si/arhiv/prispevki-in-izjave-odmevi/174271811

I must specify that "Yugoslavia" can have different meanings. Thus, the period of the so-called first Yugoslavia, that is, the Kingdom of Serbs, Croats and Slovenes, which was changed to the "Kingdom of Yugoslavia" in 1929, and existed from 1918 to 1944, may be included on the list. Nevertheless, the word "Yugoslavia" is usually used in both every day and academic language to refer to the so-called second Yugoslavia, that is, the Socialist Federal Republic of Yugoslavia, SFR Yugoslavia, or simply SFRY. The frames of its existence are usually defined as the period from after 1945 until the wars in the former republics of 1992. The third Yugoslavia may also be found in different types of literature; it is used for the identification of the political union of Serbia and Montenegro or the State Union of Serbia and Montenegro, which existed from 1992 to 2006.

The period that was chosen for my research includes the socialist period, thus, the second Yugoslavia, or we may call it the period between two waves of wars: from the end of World War II until the Balkan wars of the 1990s.

The main goal of our research is to discern the key narratives implemented by museums to display the history of the country of the socialist Yugoslav period. The ways and styles of the narration were analyzed with the visual analysis method. Visual analysis was conducted during November 2013 and enriched in the following year.

As for the countries, we have selected the following capital cities for the visit:

- Zagreb, Croatia
- Sarajevo, Bosnia and Herzegovina
- Skopje, Macedonia
- Pristina, Kosovo
- Podgorica and Cetinje, Montenegro

The list of museums that we have observed consists of the following units:

Macedonia

- Museum of the Macedonian Struggle
- Museum of Macedonia

Kosovo

- Kosovo Museum
- Independence Museum [Kosovo Independence House "Dr. Ibrahim Rugova"]
- Ethnographic Museum [Muzeu Etnologjik Emin Gjiku]

Montenegro

- Podgorica City Museum
- Historical Museum, Cetinje

Bosnia and Herzegovina

- Historical Museum of Bosnia and Herzegovina

Croatia

- Croatian History Museum
- Zagreb City Museum

These museums were chosen because they were the central history museums in the capital cities. Wherever there were museum departments of contemporary or recent history, they were observed as the primary spaces for the analysis. In other cases, when such division was not available, I visited museums that accumulated the "whole" history of the country.

I have chosen the visual analysis method as being the most applicable for the purposes of my research. The essence of this method is closely related to the logic of the selected theory: understanding the context and not taking fragmentary objects for analysis. While each museum will present its national or other specific views of the researched event, discerning the same elements (statements, adjectives by which the viewpoint is formulated) and having the ability to compare them is the basis of the research. The elements of observation as the background of visual analysis aided in making a description of the visual components of the museum.

The political content of the visual data is viewed by me as a precondition for creating the national, transnational, or local identities. Therefore, it is necessary to briefly present several definitions dedicated to an understanding of the given issue.

I have described how I'm going to do my research, mentioning the methods as well as the reasons for choosing museums as the space for research. I have described several important definitions that would be useful for understanding the material presented in other chapters. I have yet to describe what we expect to determine at the museums. For this purpose, I have prepared a list of main questions important for our research.

The main research questions are the following:

The central question: How is the socialist Yugoslav period represented in the historical museums?

The additional sub-questions are proposed next:

Which personalities, events, and periods are chosen to represent the socialist period?

What are the general tendencies of museum politics in relation to the construction of national narratives in the contemporary ex-Yugoslav countries?

What is the dominant narrative of representation of the Yugoslav period in the analyzed countries?

Hypotheses

In my research, we intend to answer the given questions; for better understanding of the national museum politics, I have created hypotheses individually for each country by taking into consideration the differences that each of them had during both the Yugoslav period and the period of dissolution. The brief explanation of the reasons why I think such hypotheses could be seen in the researched countries is also provided.

1. **Croatia:** The Yugoslav period will be represented through the concept of national repression; Croats will be represented as the nation that suffered the most (the victimization discourse would be predominant); the Goli Otok (Naked Island) will be used as the quintessential symbol of the period.

Explanation: Taking into consideration the national movements that were systematically repressed, Croatian national history will be based on the actualizing of a mournful narrative. The Croatian Spring of 1971–72, the oppressions of Croatian intelligentsia and students that followed, the Serbian and Montenegrin aggression of the 1990s toward territories in Croatia and the Croatian minority in Bosnia and Herzegovina: the whole historical period of Yugoslavia will be presented as a repressive project. Goli Otok will be used, primarily because it is located in Croatia and, secondly, because it fits the narrative of suffering.

2. **Bosnia and Herzegovina:** When I visited museums located in Sarajevo, I expected to see a unified view; however, we were entirely aware that alternative interpretations would be visible in museums of other cities (e.g., Banja Luka or Brcko, or Mostar). (1) Yugoslavia will be divided into two periods that will be set in opposition to each other: before Tito's death and after. (2) Yugoslavia before the 1980s will be represented through the discourse of multiculturalism. The Bosniak identity will be given as an example of successful integration of different nations inside the federation. (3) The last decade of its existence will be represented through growing Serbian nationalism and economic instability, which will be the main factors of the explanations for the further Siege of Sarajevo and the conflicts of the 1990s.
3. **Montenegro:** representation of the "brotherhood and unity" narrative; the period of the 1980s with its growing nationalism will be avoided and not represented at all.

Explanation: Montenegro became an independent country only in 2006 when its union with Serbia collapsed. Consequently, with a pseudo-defensive rhetoric, it has to reorient its political ideology and create a new understanding of the previous two decades as part of an aggressive force. The recent past is still the matter of discussions and a harmonized national interpretation of this period has not yet been produced.

4. **Kosovo:** The representation will emphasize the elements of Yugoslav authoritarianism. The suppressed Albanian student protests in 1961, as well as the weak economic situation and growing Serbian nationalism of the 1980s would be used as key topics.

Explanation: Kosovo has been actively involved in the nation-building process since its recognition as an independent country. Being the former

Yugoslav republic with an Albanian majority, it takes Albanian history as its starting point. The area that has dramatically suffered from being part of Yugoslavia will confront the entire Yugoslav discourse.

5. **Macedonia:** The exhibition has to balance between glorifying the Yugoslav period associated with a stable economy and relative security, while finding the arguments why Macedonia preferred to become independent in such a situation. The period after World War II will be used to show the reconstruction of the country and the spirit of the collective ideology.

Explanation: Yugoslavia played a sufficient role in creating and fixing the Macedonian identity as opposed to Bulgaria and Greece, which were not part of the federation. Since Macedonia did not have a strong, controversial collective memory of World War II like Croatia and Serbia have (no local "Chetniks," no "Ustasha"), the post–World War II period could be easily used as a non-conflict one and as the period when the country was exposed to economic development and urban reconstruction.

I hope to conduct research that will not only describe the displays but also will help to find the deeper knowledge hidden at the expositions. In the next parts of the study, a brief historical review of Yugoslav history would be presented. For these purposes, the description of the decades is being used. The description begins with the postwar period (1945) and finishes with the last decade of Yugoslav history: the end of the 1980s. The most important sources for the historical part are derived from the works of Ramet (2005, 2006), Malcolm (1996, 1998), Bartlett (2003), Hupchick (2002), and Luthar (2013).

Chapter 2 presents museums as fields of social research. It sheds some light on the definitions and describes briefly the history of the development of the given institution, its purposes and ways of influence on creating cultural inequalities in different societies. This chapter emphasizes the role of museums in the contemporary world and presents the results of empirical research dedicated to the visitors of the museum. The works of the following authors greatly influenced the writing of this chapter: Appadurai and Breckenridge (1991), Bennett (1995), Kavanagh (1996), Crane (2005), Ostow (2008), Ernst (2000), Guha-Thakurta (2004), Crooke (2004),

Duncan and Wallah (2004), Wilkening and Chung (2009), Wilson (2001), Williams (2007), and Bleich (2011).

Chapter 3 represents the methodological part of this study. It is followed by the empirical part of the research, where analysis of each museum and each country is being conducted. Afterward, the outcomes from the national perspective are combined together in order to generalize the characteristics that unify the Yugosphere or distinct cases from each other. The visual analysis is accompanied by the photos made in each of the museums and helps to provide clearer visual confirmation of the extracted dominant discourse.

2 THEORETICAL FOUNDATIONS

In order to begin with the empirical part, it would be beneficial to describe briefly the main terms commonly used in the given research. Among the most important are "collective memory," "politics of memory," "museum politics," and "representation." It is followed by the basic examination of the phenomenon of nostalgia and Yugo-nostalgia. The section starts with a brief description of the concept of memory and move toward the concepts related to it.

2.1 Definitions

Memory as an interdisciplinary phenomenon integrates highly diverse elements and does not become irrelevant for many decades. The practices of remembering and forgetting, as such, and reflections on its nature, structure, transformation, and diverse applications turn out to be all-encompassing interdisciplinary social phenomena. Memory has become an important topic in politics and public discourse. It is instantly present when we refer to the context of national, local or transnational tradition, myth, and history. Memory also occupies the central sphere of human life. In everyday life, for instance, it happens in the form of the thriving heritage industry. The preoccupation with memory is visible all over the world; the "memory boom" has become the central characteristic or even diagnosis of contemporary societies. Cultural remembering has always existed, but what makes it a new phenomenon is the facts that discourses on memory are increasingly linked across the globe. Memory is related to a list of phenomena that is growing. Therefore, some scholars are focused on such aspects of memory studies as amnesia and social forgetting (see Huyssen 1995), the dynamic of cultural remembrance (see Rigney 2005), and others.

Keeping memories alive is in line with the contra-phenomenon of forgetting. Paradoxically, in the process of experiencing our reality, we, as a rule, forget things more often than keep them alive in our memory. Therefore, the following definition seems to be relevant for the beginning: "Memories are small islands in a sea of forgetting" (Erll 2011, 9). No doubt, such a brief definition does not include important factors of the process of memorizing, its selective nature and specificity relevant for diverse discourses. Nevertheless, it shows the importance of such aspects as amnesia, oblivion, and silence. In application to our study, such elements become extremely important while being the flip side of the narratives that we analyze in the history museums.

The polysemous concept of memory has an important distinction: collective memory, which is part of the puzzle and to some extent less metaphoric and perhaps more precise in definition. I understand **collective memory** to be a result of reduced, selected, and homogenized understandings of the past constructed in the process of the interaction of the individual and the intermediary institutions. Museums, in this regard, are institutions that visualize the selected form of collective memory as a signifier code and fix it in a cognitive landscape of the visitor with different dynamics of cultural remembrance. The differences in perceptional dynamics mean that the variations in the level of the habitualization of the "messages" that were provided by the narratives were instantly included into the visual representation of the exhibitions. It has to be noted that the collective memory does not have the quality of universal inclusivity and usually is competing with other sets of collective remembering. For instance, the narrative presented in the national historical museum may be totally different to the ways of interpretation of the same historical period in the parallel institutional structures in other countries, cities, or the same city. The system of relations for the past being produced through the two-sided process of the construction of common knowledge, in which the individual and the intermediary institutions are making this social reality together, form the sets of collective memory that then have a chance to be visualized through the museum spaces. Therefore, the narrative provided by the museum must not only exist but also have some visible representation in the form of artefacts and supporting description. Our goal is to find such elements that form the narrative and to perceive the collective memory narrative to which it is referred.

The term "social memory" is multidisciplinary and is used in a wide range of scientific fields. Pierre Nora used it to apply to historical knowledge, and Novick used a similar vision. Maurice Halbwachs applied it in sociology, Cole in anthropology, Schudson in media studies, Middleton in psychology, and Fussell in literature. Along with the given term, several other terms with similar meaning are used. Thus, Halbwachs calls it "collective memory," Bodnar "public memory," Seixas "historical consciousness," and one can also find other synonyms, such as "cultural memory," "historical memory," and so forth (Olick and Robbins 1998).

The given term is used in different approaches.

The first approach (chronologically) is the structural-functional approach. The aim is to study the collective's memory function, which helps the group to be integrated. The presence of common memory allows combining and giving it the necessary stability and awareness of its own integrity. Perhaps the most prominent representative of this approach is Maurice Halbwachs. He is known as the most influential theorist of collective memory (Crane 2000, 6). In the context of this study, I would like to stress Halbwachs's postulate that all individual memories rely on the "framework of collective memory" for their articulation. "Although individuals hold personal memories, their remembrance and expression depends on the changing context of the multiple communities and times in which individuals live" (Ibid.).

The phenomenological approach presented in the works of Husserl, Shutz, Ricker, Berger, and Luckmann aims to establish a correspondence between the supply of the social memory and the life world of the person. In this approach, one will find the direct interaction between the individual and other forms of the common memories, which have a social character. Social memory creates conditions for the successful continuation of communication and is typical of each social group.

The structuralist approach is represented by Levi-Strauss, Foucault, Lacan, and Barthes. It has a similar methodological background as the cultural-semiotic approach and mainly focuses on the consideration of timeless structures that permeate all layers of social reality.

The post-structuralist approach considers the dynamics of the transformation of social phenomena (including social memory) in the spatial dimension, which suggests the formation of the concept of the "topology of the social memory." Baudrillard, Derrida, Bourdieu, Foucault, and Nora might be included on the list of representatives of this approach. Thus, when discussing museums, Nora points out that museums and monuments emerged in the late nineteenth century as "sites of memory," because collective memory no longer functioned in an organic or natural way (Crane 2000, 6). Kavanagh points out that museums are usually using official and formal version of the past called *histories*, which is "different from the individual or collective accounts of reflective personal experience called memories" (Kavanagh 1996, 1).

As a term, "collective memory" is sometimes criticized as being a poor substitute for older terms, such as "commemoration," "political tradition," or "myth" (Olick 1999, 334). Olick suggests avoiding the term because of the imprecision of its definition and bearing in mind that memory has different dimensions, both as a pre-social individual memory and its implications in the public. However, it is always the same phenomenon. Thus, national memory, acts of commemoration, and personal testimonials are examples of memory but on different levels. These different forms of remembering have different levels of importance, one of which would predominate depending on the particular case (Olick 1999, 346). Since the invention of the term "collective memory" used by Maurice Halbwachs, which was understood as the constructed and nonessential nature of the individual memory included into the social context, the understanding of the term has been significantly altered. Collective memory can be understood as a discourse about events and the ways how to interpret them. Such discourses deal with two important aspects: the selection of both "important knowledge" and that which is "non-important." Having a selective nature, collective memory is hegemonic, contentious, and politically instrumental. The political characteristics of the term significantly connect it to another relevant term: "the politics of memory."

The two terms not only have similarities because of the usage of the same world ("politics") but also because of the unsettled definition for both of them. These terms are usually used as having a meaning that is intuitively clear but, of course, such setup shows the undeveloped nature of the new vocabulary. For example, sometimes we encounter the titles of articles and even academic books that contain the given terms, but throughout the text, one will hardly be able to find a single clear explanation of the term. The term "political" is often used in our daily language. This seeming openness of the meaning helps and misleads simultaneously precise understanding of the term that we try to utilize.

I would agree with the definition provided by Lasswell, and later followed by Stocchetti, and share their understanding of the **politics** "as the competition for the control over the distribution of values in society" (Stocchetti 2011, 14). Applying such a vision of politics to the private and public use of images, the authors argue that the public use of images cannot be both politically neutral or/and socially irrelevant and always either supports or disturbs the given distribution of values (Stocchetti 2011, 14).

Another term that might also be confusing for understanding the process of distribution of values in the museums is **politics of memory**. I understand it as a strategic plan and agenda by which events are remembered, selected, and displayed. The leading role in this process is given to the way the event or certain period is constructed via political leverage and how it uses the collective memory in an instrumental way to create a politically engaged historical construct.

Similar to the aforementioned term, but with more specific focus, is the concept of **museum politics**. It is understood here as the paradigm of the interpretation and representation of the past adopted by the stakeholders of the museum who construct the image of the past in the frames of the existing public narrative(s). The product of the museum politics is the exhibition as such and the relations toward the visitor that could vary from perceiving the visitor as an active contributor in the creating of the narrative to a passive consumer.

I have already mentioned the term "representation" many times and have used it with different meanings. Two main meanings correspond to the political and the visual connotations of this concept. In general terms, **representation** means "making experiences from the past present again in the form of narratives, images, sensations, performances" (Plate and Smelik 2013, 6). Perhaps, we could propose the shortest definition: representation is the "embodied performance of the past" (Wortel and Smelik 2013, 185). The representation may mean both visual embodiments of the historical narrative and also verbal, oral, or other types of narratives that are dealing with the construction of the history. Thus, a history textbook will be the essential representation of history as well as the consumer cinema that shows "the past." Representation is always connected to the constructionist scientific paradigm, to which the idea of narrative and discursive formations belongs.

Representation is closely related to another important term **historical revisionism**, which has several meanings, one of which has a negative connotation. In essence, it means the reinterpretation of the traditional dominant opinion on different historical processes. With such a meaning, it is the process of normal development of the scientific opinion and the accumulation of knowledge. However, the given term has produced a fixed negative connotation by which it means the reinterpretation of the past that is in favor of a new political and ideological order. In this study, the term was predominantly used by the experts with negative connotations, which will be clear from the text.

Other concepts that are applicable hereinafter and require special attention are **Yugo-nostalgia** and **Tito-nostalgia**. Nostalgia is one of the multiple strategies toward an interpretation of the past. It resonates with findings from several exhibitions I have explored. Starting with some general description of post-socialist nostalgia, it follows reflections on one of its dimensions (Yugo-nostalgia).

Some findings on nostalgia

Yugo-nostalgia is evident in almost every corner of the former state (Buric 2010; Velikonja 2008; Volčič 2007) and may be included in the broader context of nostalgia as a cultural phenomenon. The given phenomenon "has become a key term in discussions of the varieties of remembrance commonly practiced and represented in contemporary Western culture"

(Radstone 2007, 112). We are observing the emergence of a new dimension of remembering throughout Europe, which might be called "the nostalgia boom." This boom is the reaction to the rapid social changes in the form of activated attempts to preserve the continuity of identity (Davis 1977, 419). According to Dames (2001), it acts first of all as a reaction to the modern crisis of identity. Identity construction is closely tied to the political dimension because the individual is constructing the imagined world of comfort and sanctuary as a reaction to the non-satisfactory contemporary conditions of his or her life.

According to Velikonja (2008, 28), the main traits of a nostalgic narrative are ex-temporality, exterritoriality sensuality, complementarity, conflicted story lines, unpredictability, polysemism, and an episodic nature.

The key element that is easy to find when describing the nostalgic phenomenon would be its episodic nature, which eventually aids in understanding the mechanism of its vitality because it gives the "green light" to use a partial image of a complicated reality and to dismiss the political background of this event (Velikonja 2008, 28).

Traditionally, nostalgia was associated with false memories and forgetting, when the individual was seeking refuge from turbulent situations (Lowenthal 1989, 21), with an abuse of history and a lack of depth (Radstone 2007, 114). It has different dimensions, including cultural, political, and economic. Nostalgic affiliation may be divided into three perspectives: (1) nostalgia as a world phenomenon, (2) post-socialist nostalgia, typical for countries of the former socialist block, with a similar modus of collective remembering, and finally (3) Yugo-nostalgia, a typical phenomenon of the post-Yugoslav countries.

Consequently, as with any other form of remembering, post-socialist nostalgia "works as a form of selective amnesia, idealizing the past by referring to the low unemployment rate and strong sense of community" (Cooke 2005, 104). It is criticized for structuring knowledge in such a way that the real problems of the existence are ignored, for instance, the problems of human freedom, lack of transparency, or antidemocratic rule (Cooke 2005, 104).

When generalizing the features of the second dimension, that is, the post-socialist nostalgia, Boyer (2010) defines five main characteristics of them:

1. Nostalgia is heteroglossic.

Boyer uses Bakhtin's term to stress the plurality of images and ideas that ground the nostalgic discourse(s). Not all of them homogeneously deal with a grief for, or an obsession with the past, but rather "represent the dialogical gossamer of idiosyncratic references, interests, and affects that are channeled through nostalgic discourse" (Boyer 2010, 20).

2. Nostalgia is indexical.

This means seeing nostalgia as an indexical practice, the process of the on-going identification of the person with the world in which one had previously lived with an accent on the collective memory experience (personal versus collective identification).

3. Nostalgia is allochronic.

The given phenomenon is not only spread in one region (Eastern Europe), and is not only the product of local actors, but also the constructions provided by the postcolonial thinking of former empires.

4. Nostalgia is symptomal.

Nostalgia is a living trend in many countries and is symptomatic of contemporary societies.

Svetlana Boym identifies two types of nostalgia: restorative and reflective. The first "category of nostalgic does not think of themselves as nostalgic; they believe that their project is about truth. This kind of nostalgia characterizes national and nationalist revivals all over the world, which engage in the anti-modern myth-making of history by means of a return to national symbols and myth" (Boym 2001, 41). Restoration (from restaure, reestablishment) signifies a return to the original stasis (Ibid., 49), where reflective nostalgia's focus is "on the meditation on history and passage of time" (Ibid.). In the empirical part of our research, we will be able to observe what kind of nostalgia is represented in the exhibitions on Yugoslavia, but before moving to the analysis, we would like to introduce some findings on the Yugo-nostalgia phenomenon.

Some findings on Yugo-nostalgia

The bars and restaurants spread throughout the territory of the ex-Yugoslav countries that are decorated in a socialist aesthetic, with particular reference to Yugoslavia as a key structure of their design concept, are one of the examples of Yugoslav nostalgia. Such are the cases from Sarajevo (Velikonja, 2008), Podgorica, or Ljubljana (Boym 2001). The hotels or hostels decorated in similar styles and rock bands using the Yugoslav context for their songs (Volčič 2007, 33) are just some of the examples collecting the activation of Yugoslav context reactualization. The barbershop where one can order a hairdo à la Jovanka Broz or signs on the restroom in the form of Tito and Jovanka are other examples of the given phenomenon. The two main Serbian football teams still use the red star as a part of their emblem and use the socialist names *Partisan* and *Red Star*.

The geography of the phenomenon is spread through the whole of the ex-Yugoslav territories, and a single place cannot be defined as a major center of nostalgia production and consumption. Even though the phenomenon is visible in the majority of the former countries, the works analyzing nostalgia in the post-Yugoslav countries are sparse. The phenomenon was theoretically conceptualized by Velikonja (2008), its main forms were described by Volčič (2007), and its relatively new form of existence in the virtual space was analyzed by Bošković (2013) and Mazzucchelli (2012).

Analyzing the Yugoslav nostalgia, Volčič (2007) distinguishes three main aspects that reproduce the phenomenon's political, cultural, and economic fields, which usually overlap each other.

1. Revisionist nostalgia, which works as a political type of commemoration and mobilizes the image of the past as an inquiry for revision of the official interpretation of the former period and as the renewal of a shared sense of belonging. Usually, revisionist nostalgia is visible in public debates.

2. Aesthetic nostalgia, which functions as a cultural phenomenon and aims to preserve an authentic Yugoslav culture.
3. Escapist, utopian nostalgia, which is the most ahistorical of all three types: the commercial phenomenon that is based on the exploitation of the images of "idyllic" Yugoslavia.

The usage of this term depends on the context and its meaning is in a state of constant transformation. First, it was predominantly used in a derogatory sense to dismiss the public that does not support the new ethno-nationalist logic; more often, it is understood as a term describing a range of beliefs and practices of commemoration or (mis)remembering Yugoslavia (Bieber 2014, 5).

When analyzing these very eclectic, liquid, and fragmented practices of the commemoration of the former past, Velikonja discovered that some of them, if not the majority, are appealing to the image of Tito. The first and the only president of socialist Yugoslavia is the element of the nostalgia discourse that permeates the different imaginary spaces that could be classified as nostalgic. Therefore, Velikonja made a step forward in the classification of the given term and distinguished the sub-phenomenon: Titostalgia. He defined it as a nostalgic discourse on the late Yugoslav president, which consist of a series of disconnected discourses in which each adds some new elements to the contextual picture. The main peculiarity by which the image of Tito may be included in the nostalgic perception is the ironic decontextualization of the leader's image. For this reason, the real historical leader is of less interest to the nostalgic sympathizers, but rather the constructed image is valuable. Titostalgia, therefore, is dealing "not with the resurrection and conservation of a real person, but it constructs the new utopian narrative of needs" (Velikonja 2008, 130). Titostalgia is a life of Tito's image after his death, the symbolic life after the physical life.

As mentioned at the beginning of this section, the phenomenon was analyzed on different levels with the application of a broad variety of methods. Velikonja (2008) represents the theoretical conceptualization and allocation of sub-phenomenon of Titostalgia, Volčič (2007) discerns the core forms of this phenomenon, while Bošković (2013) and Mazzucchelli

(2012) concentrates on the analysis of the virtual Yugo-spaces. However, the field still lacks sufficient analysis in different dimensions, such as the ties with the political policy of the analyzed post-Yugoslav countries, the qualitative analysis with the representatives of the classified groups, the statistical data and comparisons on the number and characteristics of the given fragmented groups throughout ex-Yugoslavia, the nostalgia economy and, finally, the condition of memory policy in the representation of the given phenomenon in the public space.

2.2 Epistemological and methodological assumptions

The following chapter sheds some light on the methodological backdrop of this study and specifies the key aspects of the chosen methods.

The constructionist methodology developed by Peter Berger and Thomas Luckmann being a part of the phenomenological tradition is chosen for the study. We think that this theory illuminates the preconditions that determine the existence of the social world and the functioning of social institutions. It can be applied to answer the question of why the museums are perceived as important social institutions, as well as how knowledge is being constructed within them and transmitted to the individuals. The validity of this approach and broader, of phenomenological sociology, has been confirmed by the broad variety of authors who see it as an influential approach to contemporary research (see Burr 2003; Sztompka 2007; Gergen 2009; Lock and Strong 2010). However, there are critical observers who express doubts regarding the methodological grounds of the theory. The stumbling block is usually the understanding of the relativity of reality and values. I believe that this criticism is in fact an advantage of the chosen theory, because it means that it is verifiable.

The methods used for my research are the elements of discourse analysis, the visual analysis of data, and the expert interview. The first two methods are integrated into the broader phenomenological tradition and are seen by us as a logical continuation of the chosen methodology, because they are also based on the idea of the "constructivism" of positions and identities through discourse practices. Furthermore, I think that discourse analysis not only allows answering the question "What is represented in museums?" but also "Why is it represented?" and "How is the particular narrative being constructed?"

Discourse analysis will be accompanied by visual analysis methods. Visual analysis is a method with the potential for broad implications. Such relative freedom allows authors to use their own sociological imagination in order to create and modify the ways in which the visual material is to be analyzed. From the other side, the freedom given to design and interpret the material creates liabilities for the significance of the data and its relevance.

Next, the issue of the significance of the chosen method is discussed and accompanied by the argumentation for significance of the visual analysis for memory studies in general and museum studies in particular.

First, I would like to present the main points of the methodology and afterward the chosen methods.

2.2.1 Theory

Social constructionism does not have a unified or canonical constructionist position. Gergen (1998) states that it "rather consist[s] of [a] range of variegated and overlapping conversations and practices that draw from various resources and with varying emphases and combinations" (p. 34). Furthermore, the term "constructionism" itself remains undefined (Velody 1998, 33). At the same time, many scholars (Burr, Velody, Williams, Parker, and others) observe the great interest that these ranges of theories receive.

The constructionism theories could be combined under a single principle: the belief that society is the product of continuous transformation that is initiated by individuals. No single or central theory that could be called "constructionism" exists. It is rather a set of different theories that have similarities in the basic understanding of reality, or "family resemblance" as Burr calls it (Burr 2003, 3). For instance, Lock and Strong (2010), in their book *Social Constructionism*, include a large variety of authors on the list of representatives of this branch of social science. Among them are

Vico as a forerunner, phenomenologist authors (Husserl, Schutz, Merleau-Ponty), practitioners of hermeneutics (Heidegger, Ricoeur and other), Marxists and structuralists (Bakhtin), symbolic integrationists (Mead), the philosophies of Wittgenstein, Bateson, Foucault, ethnomethodologists (Garfinkel, Goffman), the synthetic approach of Giddens, discourse analysis, and some other approaches (Lock and Strong 2010).

Another approach to linking constructivism theories was proposed by Danziger, who divided this set of theories into two strands: "dark" and "light." The dark, Continental strand is based heavily on the works of Foucault and the subsequent wave of post-structuralism and postmodernism "with a concern for issues of power, the articulation of subjectivity, the relativity of knowledge" and implementation of these ideas through the research of colonial discourses, gender studies and subjectivity. The other, the "light" strand, is an Anglo-American tradition, which aims to crack the Cartesian tradition and to use the concept of everyday life in order to explain how discourse is done (Lock and Strong 2010, 9) In our research, we would apply characteristics relevant for both types and will not reduce the analysis to one classification.

Four characteristics that briefly describe the essential background of constructionism:

1. Meaning and understanding are understood as the central features of the human activity.
2. Meaning and understanding are viewed as the features that have their beginnings in social interaction.
3. Different ways of meaning-making are embedded in sociocultural processes, and they are specific to particular times and places.
4. Most theorists of the given tradition are antiessentialists. "As a result of this anti-essentialist sentiment, social constructionism has an uncomfortable relationship with ideas about realism, and hence with science, and is often characterized, pejoratively, for being relativistic" (Lock and Strong 2010, 7).

For my research, I have chosen the constructionism approach developed by Luckmann and Berger, which became prominent after their book *The*

Social Construction of Reality was published in 1966. They are usually associated with the development of the social constructivism theory but sometimes are also referred to phenomenological sociology. For instance, Ritzer, in his book *Sociological Theories*, uses both denotations when mentioning Luckmann and Berger (Ritzer 2010, 191, 649). The roots of this theory can be found in the phenomenological tradition and are most closely linked to Schutz's social phenomenological approach. It seems quite natural that Schutz, a tutor of Berger during his PhD studies and a colleague from the same institution, the New School for Social Research in New York, where Berger and Luckmann were working, influenced the origins of the young scientists.

Perhaps, if one would be asked to express the quintessence of this methodology or rather a slogan, it would be "the vertigo of relativity" (Berger and Luckmann 1991, 17). The problem that it raised is the feeling of doing something wrong and incorrect. As Latour (2013, 154) stated, "If it is constructed, then it's likely to be fake .... Even without the addition of the adjective 'social,' even in small doses, the appeal to the notion of construction always remains a tool for critique" (Ibid.). This aspect is problematized by Boghossian (2001), who criticizes the theory for its attempts to "*relativize* the notion of rationality" and "quickly degenerates into an impossible form of idealism" (11).

As part of the broader phenomenological approach, the constructionism theories see everyday life as the background of the human life activity. First, because each human being has typical and routinely repeating acts as the background of his or her life experience (Christensen 2008).

Everyday life consists of (1) rules that are shared by everybody and of (2) language, which is the instrument that helps to form and verbalize this world of shared meanings. We can move from the everyday life to the finite provinces of meaning, such as museums, theaters, religious institutions (Berger and Luckmann 1991, 39). Consequently, we can say that museums exist and are visited because they are perceived as places that represent some knowledge relevant to society. According to the phenomenological approach, the second reason to visit museums is to escape from everyday life with its routine order and typification (Schutz and Luckmann 1973).

Developing the theory and applying it to our scientific needs, I assert that the same mechanisms work in museums. When entering the museum building or exposition, one appears in a special place with its own meanings and rules, which are different from everyday life meanings. Usually, visitors know the rules even though they may not reflect on their nature. For example, they know that they have to buy a ticket and that they are not allowed to eat; thus, they perform the procedures mechanically (buy ticket, leave food in a bag, finish it before entering the exhibition) not reflecting on each of their further steps. Such awareness is possible because we know the rules that are shared by everyone else in our society, and we perceive the given rules to be self-evident. If the person acts differently, he would be distinguished as belonging to a special group and stigmatized. For instance, the person who comes to the museum and attempts to take a picture from the wall could be called a "thief," a "cad," "demented," or something else. He would represent the world of chaos and destruction because he does not act in terms of the self-evident social order. Social order is the continuous production of rules, which are created during the process of continuous habitualization. Simply because we have visited museums more than once, we have habitualized the standard procedure of visits and do not need to waste our time on thinking what to do when entering a museum.

With the further development of the theory, Meyer and Rowan (1977) argued that human life is based on the institutional rules that are transferred into rationalized myths and are originated through different channels, such as public opinion or the education system (Clegg, Kornberger, and Pitsis 2005, 53).

Another important mechanism that illuminates the construction of reality is the process of typifications. When we communicate with someone face to face, we give "labels" to the person, relying on the characteristics which we find as essential for us. For example, we can label the other person as "scientist," "musician," "vegetarian," "left-wing," "witty," or anything else that we, as the representatives of some knowledge, find the most important. Eventually, our characteristics could be modified, but we will constantly be using different labeling/typifications of others.

As long as institutions exist as an external reality, the individual cannot understand them through introspection. Perhaps the most crucial idea of this theory is the understanding that the objectivity of the institutionalized world is constructed by the individual. As pointed out by Reed (2005, 1622): "organizations are discursive constructions and cultural forms that have no ontological status or epistemological significance beyond their textually created and mediated existence." Applying this statement to the museum would mean that one needed to study it in order to discover the nature of the constructionism of its meanings.

Another concept that might be important for the goals of our research is the "rival schools of thought," which can emerge in the process of institutional segmentation. It seems to me that this concept is similar to competing narratives that work in different fields and are related to the discourses and domination. Each of such a system is an alternative interpretation of an event, period, or action. Its main specificity is the intention "to establish itself and to discredit if not liquidate the competitive body of knowledge" (Berger and Luckmann 1991, 103). Applying the aforementioned concept to the representation of Yugoslavia will mean that different viewpoints on the Yugoslav period will represent rival schools of thoughts. Moreover, the emergence of alternative forms of commemoration practices, such as Yugo-nostalgic parties, would be another example of such systems. Each system needs resources in order to maintain its existence. For instance, the Yugo-parties might be interpreted as events aiming to maintain and fix a particular reality. Museums would also be involved in maintaining their reality by organizing different meetings or round tables in which a particular vision of reality will be supported by experts' opinions. Thus, experts can be understood as an important element that supports the existence of the specific reality. If we take a museum in Yugoslavia as an example, the possible experts could be politicians who come on official visits, former soldiers, and veterans or any other group that came to visit the museum.

Similar examples can be found in the case of the reproduction of "Yugoslav" practices. In order to maintain the special reality and to cope with "reality-slipping," different ceremonies from Yugoslav times (celebration of May 25, flying the Yugoslav flag, etc.) are organized by the Yugo-sympathizers.

Additionally, different events, which are considered by us as such, that maintain the existence of specific reality are capable of turning "the individual from the tenuous reality of early-morning grogginess" (Berger and Luckmann 1991, 169) and proclaiming to him or her that reality has a particular set of features. It has to be mentioned that "the tenuous reality of early-morning grogginess" was applied by Berger and Luckmann to the "non-significant" day-to-day situation of riding on a commuter train, where they wanted to show that even such activities, which are usually perceived by us as unimportant, can influence the construction of individuals' vision of reality. Seems, this extremely accurate observation can be applied to our research focus. Thus, for example, the young person with a not too strongly fixed vision of reality can be influenced by train passengers who sits in the same wagon (insignificant others) and express ideas about the life in Yugoslavia as being sufficiently better than in the current time. The fixation of a good image of Yugoslavia could be finally made after a visit to the exhibition, where such image would be presented in an unambiguous manner. The exhibition will strongly influence visitors because it might be perceived as institutional and hence "objective" reality and as a verbalized form of confirmed world order.

I have mentioned insignificant others, that is, the background, a core of day-to-day reality, that can influence a person's world vision. Even more influential are, clearly, significant others who serve to maintain a subjective reality in its most influential way. These could be close relatives, friends, and other people whose opinion is important to the individual. All of them, applying our focus, would be forming the positive, negative, or neutral visions of the past.

There are no serious objections in contemporary theory that belittle the role of language. Constructionism theory is not an exception and, consequently, the role of the language together with discourse, knowledge, and culture are considered important aspects of social reality construction that "play roles in forming our dispositions and beliefs and these in turn play a key role in forming normative institutional structures" (Elder-Vass 2010, 203).

To this point, only the processes of individual's integration, mild and non-conflicting, have been described. However, what about individuals who radically change their identities because of different reasons, what about groups that can be united by an alternative vision of reality? Where can they be allocated and how can their activities be explained?

Such cases could be combined in the group of individuals who came through the process of *alternation*. For instance, converts who have changed their religious identity from being a Jew to being a Catholic might represent such a case. The reasons for such transformations can be very different—from a pragmatic profit to a deep inner decision.

Alternation can be defined as the radical reassignment of reality—the transfiguration of the individual. Defining Yugoslavia as "an alliance of Partisans and extraterrestrial intelligence," I think, can be given as an example of radical alternation. If such a definition finds a response in people's minds, the official vision of Yugoslavia will need to compete with alternative challenges for ideological domination in the public sphere. The process of competition for domination might be visible through the emergence of alternative exhibitions dedicated to the reorganized ideological order of the narrative.

3 METHODOLOGY AND RESEARCH DESIGN

3.1 Discourse analysis

My empirical research was organized with the use of discourse analysis. Initially, discourse analysis was developed as a tool that aided in analyzing texts. It was a purely philological method but, while not remaining static, the methodological boundaries were gradually eroding or (perhaps more accurately) were expanding and absorbing other scientific fields. The literal understanding of the text (book, conversation) was transformed into the metaphorical understanding of the text; the latter includes its understanding as any number of objects that can be read as a text (exposition, any visual representation). In such a way, the method transformed from language systems analysis to the broader analysis of discourses.

The given approach is based on the social constructionist methodology. The material that can be used for empirical analysis "range from media articles to interviews" (Flick 2011, 340).

Gee (2011, 17) defines seven questions that discourse analysis can actualize and analyze. We usually construct seven areas of reality with each language act and, therefore, discourse analysis is able to define them. The questions or aspects of the reality available for analysis are the following:

1. Significance

Here the main question would be: "How is this piece of language being used to make certain things significant or not, and in what ways?"

2. Practices (activities)

Here the main question would be: "What practice (activity) or practices (activities) is this piece of language being used to enact?"

3. Identities

The question for the discourse analysis would be: "What identity or identities is this piece of language being used to enact?"

4. Relationships

The central question: "What sort of relationship or relationships is this piece of language seeking to enact with others (present or not)?"

5. Politics (the distribution of social goods)

The question is: "What perspective on social goods is this piece of language communication reflecting?"

6. Connections

Here the main question would be: "How does this piece of language connect or disconnect things; how does it make one thing relevant or irrelevant to another?"

7. Sign Systems and Knowledge

Discourse analysis asks this question: "How does this piece of language privilege or disprivilege specific sign systems?"

Vivien Burr (1995) lists four important premises of constructionist theory:

1. A critical approach to taken-for-granted knowledge
2. Historical and cultural specificity
3. Links between knowledge and social processes
4. Links between knowledge and social action

The first premise means that we have to be aware that all of our knowledge of the world should not be treated as an objective truth, because any knowledge is a product of a particular way of categorizing the world. In other words, any knowledge is a product of discourse.

The second premise puts us in the anti-foundationalist precondition that the reality in which we live is changeable, and our identities and views are seen from the perspective of the constant flux of self-transformations. We understand the world in historically and culturally specific ways. Our knowledge cannot be grounded on a solid, meta-theoretical base; its conditions are not pre-given, and hence, we are living in a world of incessant transformations of views, ideas, and identities. As Chilton (2005, 23) notes, "discourse constructs social reality."

The third characteristic implies that we create knowledge through social interactions in which common trust is being constructed. The link between knowledge and social action exists through the differences of social understanding of reality, which lead to different social actions. Each action will be the result of different understandings or/and reactions to this situation.

The second methodological approach that is actively used by the discourse analysis approaches is the structuralist and poststructuralist linguistic philosophy with its idea that we always receive access to reality through language or so-called social language (Gee 2011, 58). Language is the tool that helps us to create and contribute to the construction and representation of reality. It should also be noted that discourse analysis does not limit itself solely to language analysis but extends to analyzing social life.

In order to understand what discourses mean and how their meanings are created, Jorgensen and Phillips give a flood as an example. "The rise in the water level is a material fact. But as soon as people try to ascribe meaning to it, it is no longer outside discourse" (Jorgensen 2002, 9). Some people will call it a "natural phenomena"; some will associate it with the "greenhouse effect"; others will connect the flood to the national government's failure to fund the building of dykes. There will be those who associate the flood with God's will, attributing it to God's anger over a person's sinful action. All of these ascribed meanings construct different perspectives on the same object. Each interpretation given above can be grouped into systems of similar meanings and can be understood as a discourse. In a very basic way, discourses are "the particular ways of representing aspects of the world" (Fairclough 2005, 58), specifically "the processes, relations and structures of the material world, the 'mental world' of thoughts, feelings, beliefs and so forth, and the social world" (Fairclough 2004, 124).

Closely related to the concept of discourse is the concept of representation. The way in which we show the material reflects our understanding of reality through a particular position.

From the large variety of approaches that are available today, I opted for discourse analysis in the interpretation of Laclau and Mouffe. In the following chapter, I aim to present the most important concepts and their definitions.

This theory is based on the poststructuralist principle and understands the social world as an unstable and unfixed number of meanings that are produced through language and constructed through different discourses. The different discourses represent particular ways of talking about and understanding the social world. All of them are involved in a constant struggle with each other and with the same goal: the achievement of hegemony, which is understood as the need to fix the meanings of language in their own way. Discourses can exist in a clear, defined form and may be called narratives in such situations. I follow the definition of the narrative provided by Hinchman and Hinchman (1997) and understand narratives as "a discourse with a clear sequential order that connects events and in a meaningful way for a definite audience and thus offer the insights about the world and people and/or people's experiences of it" (cited in Richardson 2007, 241).

The most important concepts that will be used in the empirical part are "articulation," "nodal points," "the field of discursivity," and "closure."

If discourse is understood as the fixation of meaning, this fixation must have elements from which it is constructed. These elements are called *moments*. The most important moments that construct the discourses are the *nodal points*. "A nodal point is a privileged sign around which the other signs are ordered" (Jorgensen 2002, 26). Jorgensen and Phillips give an example from medical discourse in order to clarify these concepts. They point out that usually the body, illness, and treatment are divided into parts in medical research, and the function of the doctor is to correctly describe the relations between these three parts. The body is not seen as something integral, but rather as split into parts that are to be treated separately. The causes of illnesses are usually seen as local and need to be cured locally. The nodal point in such a vision is "the body" because other elements are organized around it. The other elements, such as " 'symptoms', 'tissue', and 'scalpel' acquire their meaning by being related to 'the body' in particular ways" (Jorgensen 2002, 26).

The *field of discursivity* is another concept that needs to be emphasized. It means that meaning of signs excluded by the specific discourse in order to create a unity of meaning. It is everything that was left outside the discourse (Laclau and Mouffe 1985, 111). For instance, the discourses about alternative methods of treatment are excluded from the medical discourse. In the Western medical tradition, the body does not receive the meanings that it has in healing practice or acupuncture. An exposition that aims to create a positive image of the country would avoid representing information about its violation of freedom of speech, ethnic conflict, and so on.

Elements are the polysemic signs whose meanings have not yet been fixed. They are multiple and have potential meanings (i.e., they are polysemic). Each discourse is based on the technology of the transformation of the polysemic signs into signs with particular meanings. Such elements are called *movements.*

A museum's exhibition can serve as an example. The exhibition dedicated to Yugoslavia is usually predominated with the particular representations of meanings: positive or negative. The same element lost its "surplus meaning" by being included in the chain with other elements in different exhibitions. For example, a neutral element, such as a table, receives its prevailing connotation (positive or negative) by being placed in the exposition dedicated to political repressions. From the object that potentially has hundreds of meanings, the table is reduced to one meaning. It would be the object that was used by representatives of a system to convict people. It should be mentioned at this point that usually the object does not have a separate meaning or particular focus but is perceived as being a part of a broader picture. When the object is placed into a particular context, it becomes a moment (a sign with fixed meaning). The field of discursivity is the concept that reminds us that the object could have meant something else (was an element but not a moment) before being placed in the given exhibition. For instance, if being put in an exhibition dedicated to a famous writer, the table would signify the place that served for writing famous and significant texts.

Any practice that transforms elements into the moment is called *articulation:* "The emergent discourse brings together into a particular articulation the italicized elements which can be seen to emanate from a variety of prior discourses, which are found separately from each other elsewhere, but brought together in a distinctive way in the body of texts represented here" (Fairclough 2005, 61).

"It establishes a relation between elements such that the identity of the elements is modified" (Jorgensen and Phillips 2002, 28). For example, if we use the formulation "body and soul," likely we are appealing to the religious discourse where (as in any other discourse) some meanings of the object are put forward and others ignored (Jorgensen and Phillips 2002, 28).

Following the theory of Laclau and Mouffe, I have implemented it in the special field analysis of museums and would like to propose an additional term that seems to be missing from the given theory. Analyzing the exhibitions dedicated to the Yugoslav period, it can be assumed that there would be the following nodal points: Tito, Yugoslav flag, photos that represent the Yugoslav nomenclature, or mass celebrations of official holidays. These elements *per se* are neutral. Before been displaced into the particular context, these meanings are, as Schrödinger's cat, undefined.

Let us imagine that a person who holds positive images of Yugoslavia comes to the exhibition dedicated to political repression. He would see there the same attributes that are associated with his imagined Yugoslavia (the flag, a photo of Tito), but in addition to the familiar elements, he sees photos, documents, or other artefacts that tell about the dark side of the regime, that is, the repressions. In this case, articulation into a particular discourse will be produced by combining the neutral elements with uniquely negative ones. There are some elements that have received ultimately universal meanings in particular cultures. For instance, Nazism and the Holocaust do not have any alternative meaning except negative wherever they would be displayed. They are never neutral; they can always be used as a symbol of inhumanity, as a symbol with negative connotations. The denying of the Holocaust or attempts to give a positive image to Nazi regime stigmatizes and marginalizes a person. It means that an unambiguous relation to the subject has been produced. Therefore, the elements have not always been neutral before being transformed into moments, but they would be associated with negative or positive signs per se. We would agree that the swastika received its mainstream connotation in Western civilization only in the twentieth century, but in other discourses it could have other meanings, such as a symbol of fertility. However, "civilized" or "educated" person will know that one of its connotations is negative. I propose to call such elements, which are closely associated with a particular image (negative or positive) *root elements*.

A description of the theory's concept of *floating signifier* should be mentioned. These are the objects of struggle over meaning between competing discourses. It means that the same sign can obtain another meaning and, hence, can be interpreted differently if put into another discourse (Laclau 1990, 28–29). For example, a collection of knives could be perceived as an artefact of cultural heritage that performs a diversity of ornaments or a uniqueness of techniques and materials. The same object in another exposition or more broadly in other discourses would be perceived as an instrument of torture and cruelty. Its meaning will vary from the contextual range.

In this study, I hope to analyze what images are competing in different museums and how they create the particular discourse in the representation of Yugoslavia.

When analyzing a museum apart from other museums in the same country, we determine its dominant discourse. Ultimately, it would be positive or negative regarding the time that it describes. The next step is to compare the collected discourses and to identify the most explicit images that were produced in all of these museums. In the case of using the designated two-step method, we are benefiting from having a broader picture and may see concrete mechanisms of discourse formation as well as a struggle with similar elements in different museums for the domination of meaning. We will be allowed to see how special meanings are created from the neutral objects being included in the composition. In this way, we will be able to determine the existence of *competing discourses*.

The central goal of the chosen methodology provided by Laclau and Mouffe may be formulated as the need to understand how the discourse is being formed. In other words, how the specific reality is being constructed, so that later such a reality is determined by us as being objective. It is important to underscore that within the frames of the given methodology, the process and the mechanism of construction of the "objectivity" are of greater importance than the detection of "objective reality." It is important to take into consideration the possibility of the discourses to transform and not to be fixed. As Gee (2011, 37) states, "Discourses have no discrete boundaries because people are always, in history, creating new Discourses, changing old ones, and contesting and pushing the boundaries of Discourses."

Following the chosen methodology, the task of my research is to analyze how certain elements of the museum space are being transformed into different discourses, which compete with each other.

It was already mentioned that discourses compete with each other. In the case of the empirical research, are we able to prove or refute this? If the Yugoslav period is presented differently in different museums, does it mean that they have the same audience that has to be convinced of the validity of one of those exhibitions? Or, if there is only one way of representing history, does it mean that alternative opinions do not exist? In such a situation of monosemantism, does it mean that the society has passed the stage of collective memory confrontation and has produced a balanced reflection? When applying the discourse analysis methodology, the answer to the given questions will be yes, no, and/or maybe. According to the following methodology, the existence or popularity of a single view requires its temporal *dominance*, which means the existence of the perpetual struggle in each discourse. The usage of these concepts reminds us that the chosen form of discourse analysis reinterprets and uses other foundational theories, not only constructionism but also Marxism (with its concept of struggle) and Gramsci's theory of hegemony.

Hegemony can be defined as the *organization of consent.* Or, as Barrett (1991, 54) accurately formulates: "the processes through which subordinated forms of consciousness are constructed without recourse to violence or coercion."

People usually act as if the "reality" around them is stable and unambiguous. They are used to thinking that the whole of society and their identity are objectively given facts. Discourse analysis disputes this and claims that society, language, and identity are never totally fixed. If we do not have a completely fixed reality, all we can do as scientists is analyze the ways in which we create the fixed reality that appears to us as an objective one. In this context, society is not possible (Jorgensen and Phillips 2002, 38); more specifically, society is possible only as an incomplete form, as the form that always exists in the form of eternal transformation. Discourse analysis may help analyze how social reality is reproduced and how the power relations that reproduce the social order are constructed (Paltridge 2008, 180–181).

The example of the relativity of our perception can be demonstrated by our attitudes toward children. Today, it is obvious to us that children are a group with distinctive characteristics. Hence, we perceive the discourse about children as a matter of course. However, several centuries ago, children were perceived as small adults with all consequences that this vision brings. Such discourses that were strongly rooted can be called *objective.* The concept of hegemony, which was mentioned before, helps to understand the mechanism of such objectification because it is located somewhere between *objectivity* and *politics.*

If all meanings are fluid, and all discourses are contingent, then the hegemonic discourse presented as the objective is disguising the alternative possibilities of interpretations and representations. The hegemonic discourse that is equal to objective reality is ideological in its nature, and, hence, such objectivity is also ideological. Scientists who are trying to identify the ideological narratives have to deconstruct them by analyzing what issues are not included in the discourse (Paltridge 2008). In my particular case, the analysis of not-represented issues in museums gives us a chance to deconstruct the hegemonic discourses, to determine what is leveled.

Discourse analysis will be implemented through the use of terminological systems and transformations of the material into discourses with further descriptions of them. Technically, it is expected to analyze the material through the visual analysis and thereafter to determine and convert the received material into discourses.

In my case, I will focus on a visual communication analysis. The ways of the representation of the social actors may be seen as the applied possibility of the discourse analysis. Leeuwen (2008, 140) suggests analyzing images through such elements—visible elements in the photos—social distance, social relation, and social interaction. The first help to understand how close or far the person or object in the photo is located; the second is analyzed through the power over the viewer, the equality with the viewer or the absence of such power; the social interaction may be analyzed by looking into a person's eyes: does he or she look at the viewer or not? In the first case, the interaction would be defined as direct, in the second, as indirect (Leeuwen 2008, 141).

Heretofore, we've described discourse analysis and further would like to introduce the second method of our research.

3.2 Visual analysis

The visual is an integral part of contemporary social life. It is almost impossible to imagine our life without visual advertisements, films, the Internet, SMSes, graffiti, monuments, computer games, clips saturated with visual images, or the stylized "street" of the supermarket (Sztompka 2007, 6). The ranges of the methodologies that are focused on the analysis of photographic images are the main element of visual culture, whereby the main approaches are included into the framework of cultural studies (Tister and Wells 2008, 63).

Today's society is more visual than previous ones were (David and Sutton 2011, 428), the explanation for which lies in the appearance of photography and film. As a result of common social practice, many scholars are arguing that visuality possess central place at the sociocultural construction of human life in contemporary Western societies. Such an accent on visuality is called ocularcentrism (Rose 2001, 6) and is often related to the broader transformations of modernity into postmodernity (Ibid.).

Visual analysis represents the broader directions in cross-cultural and interdisciplinary research, such as visual sociology. In short, visual sociology is interested in different visual manifestations of social life, everything that could be noted visually and, hence, photographed. Visual data are understood as "any kind of visual material, either produced by actors (such as lay photographs) or social scientists (such as video records of social interactions) that depend on the meaning and significance of the visualized records, be it diagrams, photographic reproductions or videotaped records" (Knoblauch et al. 2008).

"The central aim of the 'cultural turn' that is visible in social science is to argue that social categories are not natural, but instead are constructed" (Rose 2001, 11). Such constructions can also take visual form and, therefore, can be analyzed as any other element of social reality (Ibid.). Rose emphasizes three terms that we consider as important for our study: visionis, visuality, and the scopic regime.

Visionis is what the human eye is physiologically capable of seeing (although it must be noted that ideas about that capability have changed historically and will most likely continue to change). **Visuality**, in contrast, refers to the way in which vision is constructed in various ways: "how we see, how we are able, allowed or made to see, and how we see this seeing and the unseeing therein." The scopic regime is similar to visuality and means "the ways in which both what is seen and how it is seen are culturally constructed" (Rose 2001, 6).

Not only do different historical and political regimes have different visual saturations, but the same is also applicable to different contexts of social life: family, educational, religious, professional, and entertainment (Sztompka 2007, 15). All contexts and visual manifestations of social life may be the subject of the photographic record and, once fixed, they receive the possibility of becoming data for analysis (Ibid.). In order to fix the image, a researcher needs to use the observation method and develop the visual imagination. Nevertheless, I would like to emphasize that using the visual methods as a single method for my research will not bring objectivity to it. I stand in solidarity with Banks, who recommended using visual images as an additional value within broader sociological research enterprises. In such cases, "the overall theoretical frame of the research project will influence the orientation taken towards any visual images encountered or produced" (Banks 2001, 178).

In the middle of the twentieth century, the photo started to be used as material for social analysis; first, by the anthropologists who were using photography as "a visual notebook to document aspects of society" (Martin and Martin 2004, 12). However, photography as an object of research began to be used much later. The example of classic research may be associated with Erving Goffman, who analyzed 508 photos from different sources of mass-cultural production that provide us with images like advertisements. A researcher discovered the different forms of expressive behavior typical for representation of men and women. Women were usually slightly lower than men, who were located behind them; it was more typical for them to sit or to lie down while for men it was more typical to stand. Goffman summarized that being a man or a woman is just to imagine themselves coordinated with religious notions of femininity or masculinity (Sztompka 2007, 26).

The sociologist has to be aware of the simple mistake of quantity being viewed as a quality and the requirements of the classic sociological research being neglected (Harper 1998, 29). For instance, National Geographic photographers routinely shot hundreds of rolls of film, 3,600 separate images per day and "creating so much information tricks one into thinking one has created knowledge" (Harper 1998, 29).

Photography has also actively been used in ethnographic research; the photo becomes the classic instrument, first to analyze and afterward to justify and confirm the results. However, in contemporary cross-cultural studies (in different fields of sociology, ethnography, and others) the usage of photography is expanding with other visual instruments, such as the video camera. The new challenges allow the development of new methods; nevertheless, all of them are developing in the framework of the same paradigm: visual methodologies, such as visual ethnography (Shrum and Duque 2008, 349), visual sociology, or anthropology.

Methodologically, in order to analyze a photo, the researcher needs to understand to which contexts it refers. Location influences the perception of images. Museums are one of the public spaces that have its own "modes of perception," in the words of Gillian Rose. "The same objects in the museum and in the attic will have a different meaning and a different rank" (Sztompka 2007, 9, my translation). The context dependence of the image was emphasized by Banks with regard to the process of association of certain visual images with certain meanings (Banks 2001, 10). In addition, a table that describes the characteristics of different contexts has been included to this study.

In my research, I propose using a photo for analyzing the objects. Moreover, objects that are meant to be visually consumed will be analyzed. This situation eliminates the problem of the objectivity of the photographs and the agreement of the actor to be located in the photo.

There exist two types of observations that request the use of the camera for scientific purposes: spontaneous, open and nonstructural observation, and selective and focused (Sztompka 2007, 55). In my case, I will use the structurally focused type of observation. Preliminarily, I have chosen the research destinations: museums. All museums except the national museums located in the capitals of the former Yugoslav countries were excluded. If the historical museums are not available for different reasons, I will expand my possibilities and may visit other types of national museums. Such a manner of selection allows us to make balanced research with the relevant homogenized indicators.

Photography is by itself the element of social reality: it is created by people, it represents the social life, and it is the subject of social life (Sztompka 2007, 78). When analyzing photography, three main approaches to interpretation are usually used: hermeneutic analysis, semiotics, and discourse analysis. Hermeneutics helps to take into consideration the person who was making photos. Discourse analysis helps to analyze how the same object will be understood in different discourses. It also allows determining the different ways of reading the photo. For instance, a photo of Tito in the café and another in an office may put different connotations on the images.

If the image becomes the object of research, the semiotic or structural approach may be applied. The photo is understood as a sign or as a system of signs with the meanings relative to the given society. Following the typology of signs proposed by Charles Pierce, signs may be divided into three categories: icons, indexes, and symbols. The icon is the simplest and most neutral of the three elements. It simply denotes the object without giving it any social or cultural meaning. If by depicting the icon or putting it into a broader context there are intentionally additional connotations, it would then become an index. For instance, the sofa becomes an index the moment it is meant to mean comfort, evening hours, psychological therapy, or any other social construct.

Finally, a symbol may be understood as a sign that denotes the object on the basis of a systematic set of associations that allow interpreting the object collectively in a similar way (Akins 2006). The Wi-Fi symbol could be one such example.

If the aforementioned description provides a very basic understanding of the elements depicted in the photo, Rose (2001) enriches analysis by defining three main aspects or modalities of the image:

- Technological (material)
- Compositional ("content, color and spatial organization")
- Social ("the range of economic, social and political relations, institutions and practices that surround an image and through which it is seen and used") (Rose 2001, 17)

Another category that is often used for the visual analysis is the category of denotation and connotation, which was introduced by Roland Barthes. The main purpose of his analysis was to understand what the image represents, as well as how and what is simultaneously hidden. Denotation is the simple sign: "person," "friend," "couple," or any element. It answers the clear question: "What or who is being depicted here?" (van Leeuwen 2008, 94). Connotation is a more complicated associative array that includes the ideological determination of the context. Basically, if the denotation is the *signifier*, the connotation is the *signified* (Ibid., 95). For visual analysis, the group connotation prevails. In the given study, the images with the commonly recognized connotations would be observed.

In addition to presenting categories, one should remember the difference between the *studium* and *punctum*, concepts that Barthes also introduced. The *studium* demonstrates the interest that a person shows toward the photography in an attempt to determine its underlying meaning. The *punctum* is "the recognition of the meaning contained within the photographs" (Martin and Martin 2004, 18). Photos of the extra class that bring deep connotations are often included with the punctum. The photo of the student who is blocking a column of tanks in Tiananmen Square would be one proper example (Sztompka 2007, 88). However, when applying Barthes's tools, we have to be aware of its main applied purpose. He was concerned predominantly with semantics, that is, the meaning of the sign than with its syntax, that is, the grammatical structure of the language (David and Sutton 2011, 435).

While no single approach to semiotics exists, the one described above belongs to the French school of semiotics. Alternative approaches are found in the social semiotics of visual communication. Its main focus is on the understanding of the semiotic means or, in other words, the visual means of communication and analysis of the ways of how individuals deal with images (Jewitt and Oyama 2008, 134).

Another approach to visual analysis could be iconography. Panofsky has sufficiently contributed to the development of the given approach (van Leeuwen 2008, 100). Iconography distinguishes three main layers of the pictorial meaning: first, the representational meaning, then iconographical symbolism, followed by iconological symbolism (Panofsky 1970, 52–60). Representational meaning is similar to the denotation and means the identification of the object in the image.

Panofsky contributed to the analysis of Medieval and Renaissance paintings; as a result, two types of symbolism as layers had special relevance for the analysis. The given operational model may be still used for contemporary visual analysis. Thus, the iconographic symbolism means the connection of the artistic motifs (composition) with the concepts or themes (Panofsky 1970, 54). An example would be if one notices that the object in the picture has some symbolic message: "a female figure with a peach in her hand is a personification of veracity" (Ibid., 54). Such symbolism may be also found in the pictures or photos of popular art, in which the postmodern deconstruction creates the multilayer complex of meanings with symbolic connotations. The last layer, iconological symbolism, is the deeply rooted ideological understating of the reality that is the product of a painter's psychosocial skills that he or she might not even reflect. This may be called "more-than-visual meaning" (Panofsky 1970, 205).

At the final stage of description, I would like to summarize the main characteristics of the photo as a methodological tool. Stated briefly, the photo may perform two functions: heuristic and verification (Sztompka 2007, 102). Expanding the list, photos perform the following functions:

1. Stimulation of the social imaginations and attention.
2. Heuristic inspiration (finding of the new data through the photo).
3. Registration, descriptive inventory of visual facts.
4. A pretext for photographic interviews or discussion (for our research the given function is nonrelevant).
5. Illustrative material for presenting sociological knowledge
6. Actualization of a particular problem (the given function is more typical for art projects rather than sociological research. In the historical perspective, it was used when making the cycles dedicated to particular problems, e.g., AIDS, poverty, and marginalization. Today, the most popular topics have changed and consist of illustrating war [Tantrigoda 2013, 14] and the promotion of the ecological movement).

Visual analysis is valuable in the application within the discourse analysis (Shrum and Duque 2008, 349). In discourse analysis, the word "text" often includes images (David and Sutton 2011, 437). Gillian Rose (2001, 150) defines two types of discourse analysis and underscores that one of them focuses on the observation of some stereotypical object, person, or myth. For instance, the construct of the typical prostitute or the typical psychiatric patient is formed by a selection and simplification of criteria that describe the object.

Another type of discourse attempts to observe for whom the power is constructed and maintained through the representation. Maps might be the classic illustration of such constructs (David and Sutton 2011, 438). Here, we might take into consideration the titles that are mentioned, their visual images and connotations. On medieval maps, the objects in the center were marked as being physically bigger and, in such a way, the distribution of power was clearly articulated.

In this regard, it is important to observe the significant role of public institutions, particularly museums as an object of visual analysis. "The study of the visual organization of museums, archives and galleries ... image collections ... provides an important set of sites for the further conduct of visual discourse analysis" (David and Sutton 2011, 439). Visual analysis is the analysis of the significance of the visual itself (David and Sutton 2011, 425). The museums that we are analyzing in our research are the places of historical visuality and, therefore, their images are significant for visual analysis.

Conclusions

I have chosen the following group of instruments of empirical research because they respond to the goals of research: they help to extract the hidden knowledge from the museum exhibitions, make the dominant narratives visible, make the objects comparable, and the texture of the representation clear. Being constructive, they do not come into methodological confrontation and complement each other. Constructionist theory obtains required concepts for proper and deep interpretation of the museum's space for political and cultural perspectives. Discourse analysis gives a descriptive procedure of implementing it into empirical data.

The given methods afford flexible possibilities to influence the design of the research and emphasize the active role of the researcher in making the final intellectual product.

Additionally, as it was shown earlier in this chapter, the constructive theory of Berger and Luckmann aids in finding the conceptual answers to the applied historical questions dedicated to Yugoslavia. The given theory makes clear the reason the Yugoslav leader was of such crucial importance for maintaining the particular order and why the dissolution of Yugoslavia was possible after his death.

Thereby, the chosen methodology responds to the need for studying political component in the museums and explores the hidden sociocultural patterns there.

3.3 Museum space as an object of analysis

3.3.1 Introduction

"At the end of the twentieth century, it is difficult to imagine a literate individual who would be ignorant of the museums" (Crane 2000, 1). Particularly with this quotation, I would like to begin the chapter on museums. The statement includes three important dimensions, which would be illuminated next: periodization, imagination, education. From the current perspective, Crane simultaneously refers to the process of the formation of an image. The museum became the common marker of a socialized person, who has to visit it at least once in order to pass through the initiation for inclusion into "civilized" society. In the first chapter, the historical preconditions for the emergence and development of the museum in Europe will be presented.

The second aspect mentioned by Crane is imagination. The relation toward another as the result of constructing images, moreover, the division into the dichotomy of "cultured"-"uncultured," is the basis of the museum of the modern time. Why and how such a dichotomy has appeared will also be presented in this chapter.

The third aspect, education, can perhaps be seen as the key instrument for creating modernity as we know it. Education, viewed as a political process, in which governmental institutions and other actors are constructing national myths, history and, consequently, national identity, will also be the subject of our discussion.

Thereafter, I would present empirical cases from different museums, which would illuminate how museum analysis is being produced in modern science. Some statistics on participatory activity and features that have to be taken into consideration when researching the museum will conclude the chapter.

3.3.2 From "curiosity" to "national project"

Today, it is assumed that the proto-institutions that are recognized as museums (literally, "temples of the Muses") appeared in Europe at the beginning of the eighteenth century and were called "curiosity cabins" or "cabinets." They were made on the basis of the private initiative of those who could afford to collect and maintain unusual items. Apparently, such a habit became possible during the period of enhanced colonization. Susan A. Crane notes that the characteristic that can be extended to all the original museum "cabinets" was the fact that all of them were "results of individual efforts, expressions of the tastes and interests of a single collector" (Crane 2000, 68) and "a matter of organizers' choice" (Crane 2000, 67). All of them were the result of private taste and choice.

Crane made a retrospective analysis of how the relation to museums was changing over time and found in the texts of contemporaries, for example, by the director of the porcelain collection in the middle of nineteenth century that the "curiosity cabinet" came to be considered in bad taste and the collector was thought to be a dilettante (Crane 2000, 75). Museums were similar to department stores in that both were the examples of the bourgeois lifestyle, and both were the spaces primarily about better manners and improved tastes (Bennett 1995, 30).

The individual taste of the collector and access provided to a limited circle of people from the same class were the main features of the earliest museums. However, the perception and function of the museum were transformed over time as the image and the purposes of the government were changing. Tony Bennett emphasizes that it was not common to build special buildings for museums' needs with distinctive architecture until the late eighteenth century (Bennett 1995, 181), but "reforms in the nineteenth century transformed museums from semi-private institutions restricted largely to the ruling and professional classes into major organs of the state dedicated to the instruction and education of the general public." Museums were intended for people but were certainly not of the people in the sense of displaying any interest in their lives, customs, or other factors. Their central message was to materialize the power of the ruling classes (Bennett 1995, 109). Hence, the main idea of the museum, according to Bennett, is to promote "general acceptance of ruling-class cultural authority" (1995, 109). Bennett has employed the post-structuralism approach, in particular, Foucault to analyze the development of national museums in the nineteenth century. The main functions of the museum can be understood as an educational space whose main purpose is to turn folk into citizens by constructing national identity and linking it to the idea of progress (Ostow 2008, 4).

Ernst uses Niklas Luhmann's system theory and argues that the reason the museum appeared in the late eighteenth century was the result of specialization and compartmentalization of arts and science, which required art to be kept distinct from other discourses (Ernst 2000, 18). In his studies, he does not question the reasons that such specialization was needed, but I would argue that it was the result of accumulated knowledge, all structured as the same paradigm of Renaissance freedom as well as the "art boom," which had the same reasons to be developed as knowledge. "To display art 'as system' required a new institution .... The museum was thus to serve both as a work of art and as a monument of history" (Ernst 2000, 20).

Bennett develops his approach by referring to the Habermas theory of public space and bourgeoisie emergence and draws an analogy between "prince-vassal" relations that were transformed to "government-people" relations. "Habermas argues that during the period of absolutism, all major forms of displays, including those associated with collections, served to fashion a representative publicness for the prince: to enhance the prince's power by symbolically magnifying it in the public domain" (Bennett 1995, 33). Then the episteme (if we take Foucault's formulations) typical for the classical era was transformed into a modern one (Bennett 1995, 33). Crane also had in mind a similar idea when stating that the early modern, private cabinet collections were transformed into "the modern public museums in terms of the creation of a bourgeois public sphere in Europe, with its reforming and controlling impulses mixed with the goals of education and preservation" (Crane 2000, 3).

As an example of transformations that have accrued and have spread throughout the "civilized" world, the British Museum is a classic case in museum studies. It was founded in 1753 and "had emerged in the early nineteenth century as the exemplary metropolitan institution: a magnificent repository of antiquities of all civilizations of the ancient world. Foremost of the knowledge-producing institutions of the empire, it exemplified the idea of the imperial archive, an entire epistemological complex for representing comprehensive knowledge whose reach extended across the globe" (Guha-Thakurta 2004, 45). The museum was used as a visual invocation of a historical past, shared "the space of the greater stenographic spectacles and illusions that the century introduced as a source of technical surprise and wonder" (Ibid.). The museum contained a richly reverberating world of visual representations, including such elements as follows:

> Historical paintings, prints of ruins and architectural remains, dioramas, panoramas, exhibition pavilions, and museum displays where each image, artifact, and spectacle of the past found meaning within a novel sense of history and antiquity. The richness, pomposity and reference to the highest aesthetic values enabled the museum to assume its premier role as the most ordered and complete replication of the past, as they transformed old treasure troves and curio cabinets into scientifically classified displays of the art and antiquities, history, and ethnography of nations. By the middle years of the century, composite collections had given way to separate disciplinary museums of art, antiquities, ethnography, and natural history, each worked out as a distinct field of knowledge and opened to further divisions and subdivisions. (Guha-Thakurta 2004, 45)

Such a long passage has been quoted because it summarized in a very accurate manner the inner changes that remain relevant to the visitors of any national museum, particularly the museum of the former colony.

A new characteristic was realized in the museum: two classic groups of unequal people, the poor and women, were allowed to visit it. From the beginning of the nineteenth century, women were sometimes encouraged to attend museums. This possibility was one of the distinguishing lines between museums and other elements of the bourgeois public sphere, such as coffee houses and academies, which were still largely reserved for men (Bennett 1995, 29).

However, with inclusions of a broader population, the representatives (government or the ruling elite) brought new commitments: the educational function of the museums and, associated with it, the fixation of the hierarchies. It could be stated here that the mass culture emerged as an overall strategy of expulsion, when the imagined "low-Other" was developed in contradiction to high culture (Bennett 1995, 27). As an example of such restrictions, bans on drinking, eating, touching the elements, and dirty footwear were produced.

In order to understand what museums eventually became, and the historical museum in particular, and how it functions, we need to understand the basic constructions influencing its existence. These are well-known concepts of social and collective memory. I would start the description by providing the following introductory definition: "Memory is an act of thinking of things in their absence" (Crane 2000, 2).

3.3.3 Museums as spaces of collective memory mediation

Sheldon Annis thinks that museums embody three forms of symbolic space: cognitive, social, and dream space. The first is the primary one, including the production and transmission of knowledge; the second is the space of communicating that the exhibitions could provoke. The differences of the shared experiences would differ depending on the visitor: "for partners, a museum visit may offer a chance to discuss the new car..., a family ... could talk about their dog, and a 'singleton' might be clearing her head of much accumulated work-related rubbish" (Kavanagh 1996, 3). Finally, the dream space helps to activate creative thinking.

Another author, Kuchler, emphasizes that there has appeared a "shift from the passive notion of memory as a place where visual data are stored to be tapped when necessary, to an active notion of memory as a process correlative to and coincident with image production" (Kuchler 1991, 3). The production of images in the context of a connection with memory is the final destination of our description and will be the central issue of the following part of the chapter. While memory produces images, it cannot remain static, but it can pretend to be such in order to solidify memories' meaning (Crane 2000, 1).

However, if the information that one remembers and transfers exist, there has to be a number of things that are identified as not important or which are forgotten for the opposite reasons, that is, because they are too painful.

A range of synonymous concepts was produced that describe such qualities of the memory. Aristotle developed the concept of "mneme" and "amnesis," distinguishing the difference between the first and second as between the ability "to remember by chance something previously experienced, allowing it to resurface in the soul," and the power "to concentrate oneself fully on something," recapturing from memory that which was forgotten (Kemp 1991, 87). Further development of this distinction formed the basis of

> "conceptual pairing, such as 'Gedachtnis' and 'Erinnerung', Halbwach's memoire and history, and Benjamin's 'Eingedenken' and 'Andenken'. Roland Barth's 'punctum' and 'stadium' are along the same line. Punctum is the detail that radiates from the historical material, catching the eye and taking me by surprise; studium is something that has only an 'average effect', but on which I can nonetheless put to good use for my own purpose through diligence and knowledge" (Kemp 1991, 87).

With an eye to analyzing visual material, the researcher abidingly faces the epistemological question of what he or she sees. Visualization, representation, presence, performance (and the list can be continued), but the gnoseology of perception that the researcher is instinctively using by interpreting some objects have to be defined. Is representation a stable center from which truth can be fixed or is it the objectification of ideological order that is grounded on the basis of hierarchies and simultaneously reproducing the same hierarchical discourse in the society? The second opinion was developed by Derrida in his work *Of Grammatology*.

In order to answer the given questions, Adam Bencard (2014) offers the approach of the contemporary Dutch philosopher Runia. The latter defines presence as "being in touch" (either literally or figuratively) with the people, things, events, and feelings that made you into the person you are (Runia 2006, 5).

A rather controversial observation, but based on the fact of constructivity of the presented material, the history of the museum will lie not only in the fact of what is presented but also in the fact of how it is presented. We visit historical museums in order to see "history," but the way we see some period of time is also becoming a contemporary history. By the fact of visiting the museum, we confirm the aliveness of representation given in the museum, even if we come there to protest it. The mere presence of the narrative in the public sphere fixes it in the rhizomatic structure of the discursive knowledge. Similar attitudes would also be significant for galleries or any other institutions of representations.

A recent case from Russia provides a relevant example. On the opening day of an exposition of icons in an artistic interpretation titled Spiritual Battle dedicated to the group Pussy Riot at the Winzavod art gallery, Russian Orthodox fundamentalists attempted to block the entrance to the building and to prevent the opening of the exhibition as they claimed it presented contempt against religious feelings. The police arrested nine activists and later the exhibition was opened.[6] Precisely because of the act of intrusion with its subsequent fixation at the media discourse, the exhibition (no matter if its aesthetic value) became a popular place for visits and public discussions. The struggle against or for accessibility transformed into a message per se.

When applying the notion of amnesia to museum studies, the researcher has to pay attention to the material that is excluded from the exposition. As Crooke notes, "by selecting, interpreting, and displaying its heritage, a group can bind itself together and forge a sense of common experiences and history" (Crooke 2008, 99). "For the community-based exhibition … the purpose is always to enhance community belonging. The history on the display may be meaningful only to a selected few, others may find the exhibition exclusionary, intimidating, and isolating" (Crooke 2008, 100). This author provides the example of a museum exhibition in Northern Ireland. She emphasizes that the topic of the conflict is rarely presented at museums there. When there was such an exposition, it was criticized for including an IRA gun in a display (Crooke 2008, 91). "The scale of [the] unknown and unresolved is often mentioned as the reason why museums have not provided visitors with interpretation of the conflict" (Crooke 2008, 91). Hence, one of the possible strategies that can be found in the museums is excuses for the noninclusion of controversial material in the exhibition, a strategy that can be called "avoidance of the memory of conflict."

---

6 S nagaykoy na «Vinzavod» (With the whip to the "Vinzavod"), Gazeta.ru, September 29, 2012 (in Russian), http://www.gazeta.ru/social/2012/09/20/4782021.shtml

Usually, museums are transforming visual material into chronological sequences. Such a characteristic is obviously present in the historical museums, but art galleries are not often an exception to this. The "exposition" of the museum objects, as Mieke Bal suggests, "displays and embodies the discourse of the memorial representation that both affirms and informs" (Bal 2008). History and its representational abilities together with the possibilities to modify and create different accents and, consequently, narratives are actualizing the issue of the neutrality of historical knowledge. In this regard, the conclusions made by Thomas J. Schlereth seem highly relevant (2004, 337–342). The author highlights six "historical fallacies" based on the analysis of American historical museums:

1. History is progressive.
2. History is patriotic (author stresses that cultural nationalism is still inevitable in most historical museums). This observation is in line with that of Michele Bal, who argues that the main narrative in national museums is epic (Bal 2008, 17).
3. History is nostalgia.
4. History is consensus (museums like to present the past times as "tranquil, idyllic places where visitors would leave with oversentimentalized, utopian perspectives").
5. History is simple ("to enshrine any one version of the American past violates historical truth," diverse points, aspects of the history have to be shown).
6. History is money.

Schlereth suggests three main approaches to improve exhibitions (Schlereth 2004, 342–345):

- History should be self-retrospective (everybody and museum workers especially have to refresh their reflection about themselves, and everybody would benefit from the critical self-evaluation).
- History should be communal.
- History should be personal (he calls this method "aboveground archaeology," for which the main idea is to reflect/be interested in the history of the person).

Perhaps there are no authors in the contemporary science dealing with the topic of museums who would neglect the role of museums in creating and transmitting sets of selected facts that construct the flexible material valid for modifications or freezing. In the following chapter, there would be presented the reflections of different authors regarding the definitions of museums, as well as its role and metaphors that can be applied for better understanding of the subject.

3.3.4 Museum as metaphor: Purposes and mechanism

History can be presented as a compilation of facts, as a patriotic selectivity, but how do people who are visiting the museum feel? If visitors have personal memories about the presented period will they include the "official" versions into their vision of the event? How do people remember and why do they forget? Gaynor Kavanagh focuses on this problem and provides many interesting observations.

Kavanagh is certain that many museums privilege the formal presentation of history through the "official history," in which individual memories are left behind. He terms this "a history over memory" (Kavanagh 1996, 2). When people visit museums, they bring their life histories and memories with them. Such memories could dominate any "formal" history offered and may be compared and discussed "often on a cross-generation basis within a family group." Younger generations can assimilate the museum narrative on the basis of confirmations given from the "witness" of the period. The reasons for the successful transmission of the knowledge can be received from such oral statements like "Your Granddad used to have one like that" or they could be stirred by exclusion and absence ("Where we came from, it is not called that," "for us it was so different," "I never wore anything like that in the '40s!") (Kavanagh 1996, 2).

Sometimes galleries include the extracts of oral testimony as "sound bite" quotes on text panels. Such a method helps to create the interactivity and, hence, form a more "authentic" image of the museum narrative. At this point, it must be observed that authenticity depends on the presented material, but it does not simultaneously guarantee objectivity or balance. For example, in an exhibition presenting the Partisans, the interviews with former participants may be included, but the voices and testimonies of other groups who participated in the war will remain unspoken.

Kavanagh notes that people usually remember things episodically rather than sequentially. Such a quality of memory has its consequences and gives rise to "episodic" life narratives. People may not remember the year if it is not tied to a specific period. It would be more typical, Kavanagh thinks, to hear such statements as "when I was a boy," "just after the war," "just before Bill died" rather than "in contrast to ask people to position say the 1870s" (Kavanagh 1996, 10).

Based on this, Kavanagh presents two meanings for the word "history." The first is the individual recollections mentioned earlier. The other refers to the past in the work of historians. "Historians operate as agents of society and produce histories of service that society ... locked into professional polemics over contested readings, they have become introspective, self-critical and, at times, downright uncertain" (Kavanagh 1996, 4). Following this logic, we may understand museums as mediators of two types of histories because they have to synthesize both "streams" from below and from above.

Appadurai and Breckenridge investigate another topic related to understanding the functioning of the museum. They ponder how the museum is connected to the production of the national, local, and transnational identities. Being followers of Benedict Anderson's theory, these authors use the same markers, such as media, national education, and tourism, which in their opinion construct the identity at the museums. They understand museums as the institutions that "belong to the alternative forms of modern life associated with media, leisure, and spectacle" and are usually "associated with self-conscious national approaches to heritage, and are tied up with transnational ideologies of development, citizenship, and cosmopolitanism" (Appadurai, Breckenridge 1991, 35).

The authors point out that an institution, when producing knowledge, has to take into consideration the complex mixtures of state and private motivations, thorny transnational problems of ownership, and the current politics of heritage and identity (Appadurai, Breckenridge 1991, 44). "Museums, in concept with media and travel, serve as ways in which national and international publics learn about themselves and others." The close tension between travel and museums is understood by Appadurai through the experience of different sorts of "other," separate for museum people, local people, and tourists. Thus, the domestic dimension would be the ability to "conceptualize their own diversity and reflect on their diverse cultural practices and histories"; for tourists, it would be rather the experience of ""otherness" in more intense and dramatic manner"; for museum people, it would be the desire to "experience cultural, geographical, and temporal distance" (Appadurai and Breckenridge 1991, 44). Appadurai and Breckenridge do not specify the differences among the three groups; moreover, it seems that the group "museum people" as such, could be easily transformed into both "local residents" and "tourists" groups when needed.

The other dimension mentioned above is a correlation between media and museum. Visitors habilitate the "texts," such as advertisements about the exhibitions located in the city, classifications (e.g., the classification of the tribal as "primitive") and come to the museums with already-constructed images of national myths and heroes, received through national movies, serials, newspapers, and magazines (Appadurai and Breckenridge 1991, 45).

Of interest is Apaddurai's idea that museums explicitly help to teach visitors to be cosmopolitan and "modern"; at the same time, however, this "modernity" will always be implicitly connected to the consumption of leisure and pleasure. (Appadurai and Breckenridge 1991, 45). Consequently, leisure and pleasure are viewed as the elements of the image of the cosmopolitan identity. The given two characteristics are typically part of consumer culture, and it seems significant that authors emphasize them in relation to museums. Others share this view: Terrel also writes about the commercialization of the museums and their need more than ever before to know the preferences of visitors and potential visitors (Terrell 1991, 149).

Appadurai and Breckenridge demarcate three types of museums and three forms of cultural literacy: an ethnic-national museum, visitors are being educated in the objectified narratives of nationality and ethnicity; in art museums, they are experiencing cosmopolitan aesthetics; in commercial exhibitions, they experience the habits and values of modern, high-tech householders (Appadurai and Breckenridge 1991, 46).

Viewers or visitors are not likely to be passive and empty receivers of the cultural information contained in exhibitions and museums, but rather "they come with complex ideas what's likely to be seen, and share this knowledge with those few 'experts' who are cast in the role of explainers." Thus, the museum is characterized as not being the place of passive observation but as dialogue and interaction among the viewers. Summarizing, the authors underscore that "the museum experience has to be understood as a dialogic moment in a larger process of creating cultural literacy, in which other media-influenced narratives play a massive role" (Appadurai and Breckenridge 1991, 51).

If Appadurai and Breckenridge pay attention to how identities are being produced through the museums, Michael Fehr concentrates on the characteristic of human perception to give meanings to any material that is observed by them.

Fehr, the director of the Karl Ernst Osthaus-Museum of the city of Hagen in Germany, shares his practical experience in making art exhibitions and also provides noteworthy ideas, one of which is the concept of the "ironic museum," which he borrows from the book *The Clothing of Clio* by Stephen Bann. The ironic museum supports the alternative reading of the exhibited objects, for example, to "present them as goods stolen in the course of imperialistic war" (Fehr 2000, 47). Such new examinations could aid in the inclusion of different groups of citizens who were excluded (by being not mentioned) in the museum narratives.

Another idea that may be useful to mention is the conclusion that the conditions of human life are such that one cannot live outside the fields of "empty space of memory." We always are included into remembering and forgetting, by reflecting the past within the present, and by measuring the present against the past, according to Fehr (2000, 47). He demonstrates such conclusions on one example from his curatorial practice, when an exhibition was organized with the title "Silence," in which John Cage's piece "4 minutes and 33 seconds" was the subject of attempts at "visualization of nothing into fine arts," implemented by providing an empty room, with bare walls and several chairs in the middle. Without dwelling on the aesthetic perspectives of the applied idea (in my opinion, it is brilliant), more important is the reaction of visitors who are attempting to recall what objects were presented earlier in this room, or to identify the characteristics of the ceiling in order to give it a label of any historical period ("Art Deco" in the described example). "To be lived in, the space needs to be furnished, at least with memories," summarizes the author (Fehr 2000, 46).

Finally, when suggesting how the museum has to function, Ferh stated, "I believe that it is possible to conceptualize museums as a second-order system, within which visitor can become observers of the rise and decay of orders—to conceptualize the museum as a space whose inner organization matches what it organizes and thereby enables us to shift to a new, structural perception" (Fehr 2000, 59). It might be the essence of the researchers' idea: the observation of "the rise and decay of orders," the deeply Western point, which determines the perception of the museum as idea of the order and its constructivism abilities to be dismissed by a new type of order. Perhaps, one can find some similarity of these ideas with a statement of Jean Baudrillard, who related collecting and displaying objects to the need to bring the sense of order and control of the chaos of history. Baudrillard sees the representation of the objects as overcoming time and death and as a visualization of the idea of continuity (Ostow 2008, 4).Authors sometimes use metaphors to express the vision for a deeper understanding of the essence. Wolfgang Ernst compares museum with a theater in which each artefact plays its role; each has a stage (Ernst 2000, 18). He states that "for a long time [the] museum was not a place, but a text, occupying a position in the discursive field somewhere between Bibliotheca, thesaurus, studio, galleria, and Theatrum" (Ernst 2000, 18). He sees the task of the postmodern museum in teaching visitors to cope with information.

Some compare museums with the stage, some with the library and some, as Julia Adeney Thomas does, with the object that a mime tries to present.

"With graceful and deliberate movements, Marcel Marceau's hands can trace an invisible shape, bringing it to our mind's eye in uncanny concreteness" (Adeney Thomas 2000, 97). This is a nice metaphor; perhaps, it is worth adding that the "absence" could be related not only to the history but to the museum's representation of that history. Another author, Michele Bal, compares the museum to theater, especially with mise en scène. "In theater, mise en scène means the materialization of the text in a form accessible for public"; in a museum, "both the visitors and the objects are the actors, and it is the interaction between them that constitutes the play" (Bal 2008, 19). When discussing how to transform museums, he suggests the concept of "world memories," which he uses to interpret an exhibition of teddy bears in a Canadian modern art museum. Such a marginal topic as a toy can become a good example, however, of making exhibition material truly transnational by putting the object into the global context (Bal 2008, 17, 28).

3.3.5 Visitors

Insomuch as the analysis of the representation of the information is the main focus of this study, I attempt to understand what kind of information was accumulated and transmitted into the visual presentation. The encoded messages have to have their recipients, someone who will decode it. Although it is not analyzed who the recipient is or how he or she perceives the information, it is important to understand who the possible recipients are and what trends exist in relation to the most important player in the museum, that is, the visitor. Therefore, in the following part, material that gives some basic understanding of the scientific questions related to the role and the type of visitor behavior is briefly presented.

Analyzing literature dedicated to the research of participatory activity and to the study of visitors, it is possible to conclude that there exists a trend toward using the galleries and gallery visitors as a subject of research. There is a dynamics in humanities to excrete art museums as a dominant place for analysis. In the vast majority of cases, visual analysis methods and different interpretation methodologies are in favor of such studies, as well as neglection of the attention to the visitor studies. The majority of visitor studies by no surprise focus on the art museum visitors. Therefore, this chapter is principally filled with studies conducted in different projects related to the visitors of the galleries, but they, by no doubt, might shed some light to the understanding of visitors' profile in general.

Let us begin with the moment the visitor starts observing the exhibition. Duncan and Wallah refer to the experience of one curator who estimated "that the average visitor devotes 1–6 seconds for each of the works he or she looks at" (Duncan and Wallah 2004, 51). They were describing art museums; regarding historical museums, there is no such information, so the question of visitors' activity could be an interesting topic for research. Another researcher, Alfred Wallace, observed a similar pattern of haste by visitors in natural history museums. He complained that casual visitors usually learned less than they might because they were not able to avoid the desire to continually move on to see what comes next (Bennett 1995, 181).

If one would like to understand who the visitors are, their age and sex, the research conducted by Wilkening and Chung describes the typical American museum visitor.

First, authors determined that the most active participants are "moms," who choose what museum to visit and, hence, are the primary decision makers for one to three categories: themselves, their children, and their spouses (Wilkening and Chung 2009, 52). Moreover, the largest segment of museum visitors in the United States is "moms in their thirties and forties"; at the same time, this segment is the most critical toward the museum services with only 30–42 percent of them feeling that their needs are met by the museum (Wilkening and Chung 2009, 55). In contrast to largest and least satisfied segment comes the happiest audience, which consists of men over the age of 60 (Wilkening and Chung 2009, 55). Such an active or even key position of women might be related to the transformations that have occurred in the gender and economic spheres. "In cities that have an influx of young adults, women in their twenties are now earning more than their male peers. For example, in Dallas, the average woman in her twenties earns $1.20 for every $1.00 a man in his twenties earns"

(Wilkening and Chung 2009, 87). The reason for this is found in education: women in their twenties are 1.5 percent more likely to have a college degree than men of the same age (Wilkening and Chung 2009, 87).

Furthermore, the authors concentrate on teenagers and their needs and state that teenagers need activity at the museum; they are afraid of being bored, so the museum has to establish more interactivity for them. Moreover, the availability of free-of-charge events is a major motivator (Wilkening and Chung 2009, 70).

While visiting the museum is usually understood as a type of leisure, it was important and rather interesting to know how teenagers spend their leisure time. The author conducted an online national survey and analyzed 2,300 questionnaires received from members of Generation Y, the so-called generation born around 1980. It is mentioned that still over half choose reading as a preferred leisure time activity, but the majority of those would be women (55 percent) to only 30 percent of men; 90 percent of respondents stated that they like to hang out with their friends, while playing sport was close behind. These were followed by visiting movies, computer/Internet, watching TV/DVD, spending time with family, playing video games, reading, going shopping, and doing art and crafts (Wilkening and Chung 2009, 74). Visiting museums was at the end of the list: 12th position from 15, with 22 percent stating that they would like to visit museums in their leisure time (Wilkening and Chung 2009, 88–89). This is even more complicated if we compare the option to visit the museum among men and women, because in the research regarding middle-school students, it was shown that boys were more engaged with museums, as well as men over 60 than females of the same age. The other tendency is visible when respondents are less than 30 years old, where females would more likely be visitors of museums (Wilkening and Chung 2009, 97).

Even though it is expected that the generation under age 30 would like to see and use different kinds of electronic media in museums, the results were controversial. In several museums in different cities, people in that age group were the least likely to want to see different electronic media in museums. Visitors who were over 70 years of age were 2 to 4.5 times (the number depends on the different research conducted in different cities) more likely to prefer video and audio at the museums (Wilkening and Chung 2009, 89).

Turning to the issue related to our research, the relation to the presentation of the non-glorious and shameful moments from the past is worth mentioning. Respondents were asked about their relation to the representation of the negative events in history. The vast majority (62 percent) respected the notion to problematize and display the ugliest aspects of the past as an important part of history. Thirty percent of visitors, the majority of whom were parents of children, preferred possibility of avoiding uncomfortable issues. Less than 1 percent were in favor of not seeing any "uncomfortable" topics at the museums at all (Wilkening and Chung 2009, 102). According to another study, conducted in Great Britain, even though the vast majority of the population was interested in the past and the manner in which it affects the present, only a smaller percentage expresses such interest by visiting museums (Merriman and Poovaya-Smith 1996, 176).

Another noteworthy study was conducted by a group of researchers of the British museum studies who used Bourdieu's theory of cultural capital, combined it with the category of taste and class distinction, and applied them to research contemporary British class structures. Different cultural preferences, such as music, art, and literature, were observed among people with different sociocultural backgrounds. It is worth mentioning an aspect of study that deals with the relations of artistic taste, art gallery visitors, and class positioning (Bennett et al. 2008).

The interviewees were asked to look at two pictures (one of a modernist artist and another from a nineteenth-century English romantic landscape artist) and comment on them. As a result of these interviews, it was possible to divide respondents into three groups: confident amateurs, relaxed consumers, and defensive individuals (Bennett et al. 2008, 115).

According to the research, only 15 percent of respondents visit art museums several times a year, nearly 30 percent report going once a year or less, and 55 percent never go to an art gallery. Patterns similar to these have been found in other studies and across Western European societies

(Bennett et al. 2008, 123). Moreover, it was confirmed that the typical visitor of an art gallery is a person with higher education (Bennett et al. 2008, 123). A similar correlation has been found between those who have higher education and those who obtain original paintings. There is also a strong correlation between education and owning original paintings (Bennett et al. 2008, 125).

The marker of taste is also visible when researching preferences in art styles. The majority (47 percent) likes landscapes; this is especially so among men and older people; the lowest such preference is found among those having higher professional occupations. Impressionism and modern art are preferred by less than 10 percent of the sample (the majority of which has higher education); moreover, women more often like modern art and impressionism than men do (Bennett et al. 2008, 127). This study has confirmed not only that the disagreements about taste are class based but also that ethnicity and gender have to be taken into consideration (Bennett et al. 2008, 130). "It is also evident in the tendency for the more highly educated middle class, and especially the elite, to be far more likely to visit art galleries and have views about the quality of art" (Bennett et al. 2008, 131).

Class differences are not the only distinctive feature to be detected in museums. Another less noticeable but simultaneously more anthropologically distinct characteristic may exist in museums: the different cultural structures that form the diverse perception of the same objects.

One case study in this regard was conducted by Diana Drake Wilson among Native American Indians. All of the observers were politically active in various Native American communities, and spoke English as a first language. They visited several Los Angeles museums. Drake Wilson describes how subtle differences in the language used by the American Indians in the museums constitute fundamentally different theories about communication and representation (Wilson 2000, 115). The author intended to explore how different kinds of memory constituted different standpoints within historical narratives.

It was determined that American Indians have "material memory." They were mentioning (unexpected to the "European eyes") details about things made out of metal, or made by different cultures (baby carriers versus guns) should not stay close to each other (Wilson 2000, 119). Many Euro-Americans read exhibits like texts as a series of signs with shared meaning and as something that happened earlier, but for the American Indians, it is still the representation of what is happening now (spiritual implications) (Wilson 2000, 120). This research sheds light on the differences that visitors might have while visiting museums. It shows that there does not exist the universal way of perception.

The attention given to ethnic minorities is an important issue in museum studies. According to a different research work, representatives from this group are less likely to visit the museums. For instance, the survey conducted by Greater London Arts representatives in 1989 showed that white people were 50 percent more likely to visit than people of an African Caribbean background (Merriman and Poovaya-Smith 1996, 176).

Another set of authors emphasizes that exhibitions in the modern European and American museums, when representing Oriental, African, Pre-Columbian, and Native American art "function as permanent triumphal processions, testifying to Western supremacy and world domination" (Duncan and Wallah 2004, 52). The authors cite the Louvre, in Paris, as an example of such supremacy, arguing that it not only preserves bourgeois ideology but also affirm its continuing relevance in the contemporary world (Duncan and Wallah 2004, 59). Authors align museums with temples, churches, and shrines and certain types of palaces and think that the main function of all of these institutions is ideological. The physical dominance and monumental appearance of the given buildings signal its importance. Consequently, "museums affirm the power and social authority of the patron class" (Duncan and Wallah 2004, 52).

In order to solve the problem of European hegemony, Merriman suggests several innovations for museum researchers to open up museums for broader audiences:

1. Research should be developed that allows museums to establish the composition of the communities in their area in order to compare this with the profile of museum visitors.

2. One shall provide complementary qualitative research on the interest, needs, and perceptions of users and nonusers of museum services to communicate this strategy and to evaluate the degree of success of any initiative, once it has been implemented. (Merriman and Poovaya-Smith 1996, 180)

Merriman and Poovaya-Smith believe that such research conducted on the constant basis will lead to the successful integration of broad audiences to visit museums. Authors cite the Museum of London as an example of successful changes. When developing a new exhibition, staff took into consideration the statistic that only 4 percent of visitors were from minority communities. The museum opened an exhibition with the main accent on the presentation of the issue of immigration in London. The curators also shifted the notion of presenting issues of migration from being a recent problem to the idea that is "was as old as the city itself" (Merriman and Poovaya-Smith 1996, 180). In such a way, the "notion of what constitutes the 'Other' and 'One of Us' are beginning to blur" (Ibid., 185). A similar approach of inclusion was used at the Bradford Museum, where "Asia" was not shown as "Orientalist," but as an integrated part of a culture where "the Asian presence in Britain has its history in the sub-continent, where two cultures were closely intertwined" (Ibid., 185).

In summation, Merriman and Poovaya-Smith proposes several strategies to broaden the audience. One is to change the narrative and avoid the separation into "we" and "they" groups and to present the communities equally. Another approach toward the recognition of cultural pluralism is to organize temporary exhibitions and projects linked to a particular community. An added benefit of such changes would be "the opportunity to move beyond the local and develop an international profile for the museum" (Merriman and Poovaya-Smith 1996, 183).

3.3.6 Historical museums and world war memorials

Museums and especially historical museums are "institutions traditionally charged with displaying national identity" (Ostow 2008, 3). Ostow notes that the strongest wave of museum building since the nineteenth century is under way, "from Bilbao to Warsaw and beyond, complemented by the reorganization of existing museums, especially in Central and Eastern Europe" (2008, 4).

The given growth is accompanied by the rapid emergence of the expositions satisfying the interests of different communities and groups of interests. Exhibitions are born as the result of negotiations. As Liddiard notes, "museum exhibitions have been almost always the result of considerable negotiation" of different professionals such as designers, curators, managers, historical consultants involved in the decision-making process" (1996, 167). The result is always the selectivity of information and visual artefacts or, as Dipesh Chakrabarty perfectly put, that in "late democracies," museums have emerged as "a key site for cultural politics arising over questions of the past" (Ostow 2008, 3).

A special place among historical museums is assigned to "war museums," places that sometimes can be decisive in identity making. The next chapter will be based on analysis of common characteristics of commemoration practices at war museums. My intention to include descriptions of war museums is based on two main arguments. First, Yugoslavia is related to two wars that preceded its appearance, as well as its collapse. These wars might be mentioned at the historical museums. Second, the topic is rarely mentioned in the scientific literature dealing with museum research and requires additional illumination.

The good starting point is the research made by Paul Williams, who analyzed and compared museums dedicated to different forms of violence, including genocide, terrorism, political disappearances, nuclear incidents, and irregular conflicts. He analyzes a broad number of institutions, including the Hiroshima museum, the Chernobyl museum, the District Six museum (Cape Town), the Armenian Genocide museum (Yerevan), the Liberation War museum (Dhaka), and the Srebrenica Memorial and Cemetery (Potacari). Examples from Tallinn, Los Angeles, Madrid, New York, Budapest, Perm, and other cities throughout the world are also used (Williams 2007, 7–20).

Williams defines a museum as "an institution devoted to the acquisition, conservation, study, exhibition, and educational interpretation of objects with scientific, historical, or artistic value" (2007, 8). "Memorial" is understood as an umbrella term "for anything that serves in remembrance of a person or event." In such an interpretation, a memorial can take a nonmaterial form, such as a holiday or a song.

This author mentions that memorials and monuments are sometimes distinguished on the basis of the difference of their political function. In such an approach, a memorial signifies mourning, whereas a monument signifies greatness or valor (Williams 2007, 8). Williams thinks this division is difficult to apply because the typical noble/tragic duality is used in war museums. He points out that memorials and museums differ in their demonstration abilities: memorials can visually represent their own significance, whereas museums attempt to display history in a scientific rather than a commemorative way, and therefore, they require explanatory textual strategies (Williams 2007, 8). Nonetheless, the distinction between museums, monuments, and memorials are not concrete; the formal distinction between these designations is blurred in the contemporary tradition of commemoration (Williams 2007, 8). Consequently, he defines a monument as "a sculpture, structure or physical marker designed to memorialize" and a memorial museum as "a specific kind of museum dedicated to a historical event commemorating mass suffering of some kind" (Williams 2007, 8).

Analyzing world war memorials, Williams emphasized that they have a relative simplicity of form and help to engender and consolidate social practices of visitation (2007, 5). He also addresses interesting issue: why do people visit places that do not bring peace and harmony to the senses? What is the purpose of putting oneself in the discomfort zone? Visitors do not typically go to a memorial because it looks nice or because they hope to receive positive emotions about the subject as may happen with visiting history museums. Instead, people come there with respect. Sometimes respect can be personalized when it is loaded with familial significance. Hence, the "World War memorials act more as a staging point for mourning will and reflection than as destinations that explain the significance of an event" (Williams 2007, 6). In addition to respect, memorial museums have several other missions:

- Illumination
- Commemoration
- Education (Williams 2007, 26)

All of these functions are presented at Srebrenica. Analyzing this museum, the author points out that the museum in Srebrenica (and in some other Asian museums) "share a sense of intense brutality that was intimate and corporal, yet socially dispersed—that is, the attack occurred only-by-one .... They display what the perpetrators aimed to affect: lifelessness" (Williams 2007, 27).

The illumination of different categories of objects might produce different understandings. According to Paul Williams, there are three main object categories in our type of museums: first, victims' remnant personal effects and perpetrators' tools of atrocity; second, bones and other human remains; third, public tokens and commemorative offerings.

It is important to note that the same objects acquire the opposite connotations depending on the type of museum in which they are presented. For instance, weapons demonstrated at the military museum generally symbolize strength and national pride, while the same object placed in another context (e.g., museums of genocide) would be understood as signs of degradation, horror, and inhumanity. Furthermore, such objects will serve as a proof of atrocities made by the "other side."

Williams divides visual objects into "hot" and "cool" forms. "Hot" objects speak in an emotional way due to their capacity for personification. Personal items with their stories are related to this type. For example, a bar of soap engraved with the words "I love you" or the coats of prisoners represent hot objects (Williams 2007, 33).

"Cool" objects explain more easily the details of what has occurred. They are a kind of visual "hook." For instance, a picture on the wall that reconstructs the events and demonstrate "how it was there" can be used as cool objects (Williams 2007, 34).

3.3.7 The problem of the representation of human remains in a memorial museum

The decision to show or to avoid showing human remains in memorial museums remains open to debate. Nevertheless, the tendency to bury bodies and to avoid presenting them is increasing. There are several reasons for this. First, because of ethical reasons; second, because of the stress for visitors. Those who still use human remains as an object of exposition argue that it is evidence of what had happened, which risks being forgotten if the object disappears. Furthermore, the body functions as a confirmation for those who doubt or deny the genocide (Williams 2007, 38–46).

Others see the display of remains as unproductive and say that the main purpose of the memorial is the exchange of ideas not collections of bones (Williams 2007, 42). We would support the second group because the case of Holocaust deniers shows that no amount of evidence suffices if the person refuses to believe: documents, publications, and even the testimony of survivors. The classic example of such "revisionism" is David Irving, who states that the walls of Auschwitz's gas chambers, which he had illegally sampled when visiting the Holocaust memorial, contained no evidence of cyanide gas (Bleich 2011, 52).

Additionally, memorials always run the risk of using the dead bodies as props. In such a situation, instead of being spaces of memory, the place in transformed into a propaganda space, where death is used "as rhetoric devices" (Rev 2008, 76). In analyzing the famous Museum of Terror in Budapest, Rev came exactly to such conclusions.

3.3.8 Conclusions to the chapter

On the basis of the analysis of literature, I would like to summarize the notions discussed into three main points.

The museum is a space of ideology/-ies

Carol Duncan argues that museum expositions do not change the world and do not have to do this, but as a form of public space they construct the arena in which particular communities test, check, and live with the constructed truth and discover the opportunities of the emerging new truths.

Appadurai and Breckenridge emphasize that museums are the spaces in which (1) spectacles, (2) discipline, and (3) state power interlink with questions of entertainment, education, and control (Appadurai and Breckenridge 1991, 51). Such a mix creates the ideological product that cannot be neutral.

The museum is a political object

The institutions that are focusing on the extraction of the quintessential knowledge of the national history are simultaneously connected to the production of the political discourses by the need to select the events from the broader perspective, by the need to give connotations to them and, finally, by the need to create a monolithic and clear narrative, which is always a simplification of the historical context. According to Luke (2002, xxiv), "Museums must be taken more seriously as cultural texts and polemical locales, because political discourses have more voices in them." The exhibition, regardless of what focus it has, is always "the product of the struggle by individuals and groups to establish what is real, to organize collective interests, and to gain command over what is regarded as having authority" (Ibid., xxiv). The selection of the topics and the requirement to create the content based on the values and rules of the contemporary state order affect the representation of the material. The actualized discourses of ethnicity or hidden discourses of race are merely an example of the selection criteria that museums have to take into account. Being state institutions, they are not expected to criticize the meta-narratives of contemporary politics (such as the value of democracy, the gender rules or political system of the country, and many others). Furthermore, the need to take into consideration ongoing memory struggles that different groups have does not allow museums to be politically neutral institutions in a broader sense, while selection or refusal is becoming the political act influencing the construction of the national identity of the visitors as well as non-visitors.

The museum is a space of the intersection of past and future

It is impossible to consider the future without the past. At the same time, without understanding the future, it's impossible to "construct" the past, because the selection of facts from the past dictates the tasks for the future. Therefore, a museum is a space of the intersection of the past and future.

These three theses argue that the museum is a deeply political institution, which helps different groups to use the space in their interests. Therefore, the museum is a place of concurrences of power and meanings, and a place in which the material talks not only about the history but also about the actors, involved in creating the meanings.

4 BRIEF HISTORICAL BACKGROUND OF YUGOSLAV HISTORY

In this study, the focus of attention is the period of the so-called Second Yugoslavia. From 1945 until 1963, it was called the Federal People's Republic of Yugoslavia (FPRY); in 1963, with the new constitution, it was renamed the Socialist Federal Republic of Yugoslavia (SFR Yugoslavia, SFRY). The chronological framework includes the post-1945 aftermath of World War II until its disintegration in 1992 when Slovenia and Croatia proclaimed their independence. The Yugoslav Wars that followed are related to the disintegration of Yugoslavia and to the attempts to create the "Third Yugoslavia," inaugurated on April 27, 1992. The new (non-socialist) Federal Republic of Yugoslavia comprised two countries: Serbia and Montenegro. However, the new state was not recognized by the majority of countries because of its continued military invasions of the other republics of the former Yugoslavia.[7]

The issues related to the dissolution of Yugoslavia and the beginning of wars in Kosovo, Bosnia, and Croatia are also taken into consideration; nonetheless, the given period requires a separate study because of its great complexity.

The SFRY (hereinafter, we will call this entity "Yugoslavia" for simplicity) was formed in 1945 as a federation consisting of six socialist republics: Serbia, Croatia, Bosnia and Herzegovina, Montenegro, Macedonia, and Slovenia. Serbia included two autonomous provinces: Kosovo and Vojvodina. The first Yugoslav elections took place on November 11, 1945. The leader of the country became Josip Broz Tito, who was the leader of the Partisan movement during the war.

Before the Tito-Stalin rift in 1948, Yugoslavia could have been described as a communist orthodoxy (Allcock 2000, 271) that functioned similarly to the Soviet Union.

---

7 Britannica http://www.britannica.com/EBchecked/topic/654691/Serbia/214088/The-third-Yugoslavia

A brief historical overview will be presented decade-wise. Not all specificities of each federal unit that took place through the years can be considered. I also am aware of the fact that each national unit has its unique features due to the complex number of actors, cultural differences, geography, and international politics. However, I assume that the description presented in the form of decade order permits the portrayal of the general tendencies of the period in each federal unit, while simultaneously providing an overview of the important events happening on the national level (e.g., protests in Croatia or Kosovo). The Yugoslav period is split into four decades:

1. 1945–59
2. 1960s
3. 1970s
4. 1980s

The following chapter will briefly describe the historical period of Yugoslavia, from the end of one war (World War II) to the beginning of another (the wars in the former republics of Bosnia, Croatia, Serbia, and Kosovo). Accordingly, Yugoslavia may be considered, in a sadly ironic way, as the peaceful period between two wars. Even though the period was not as peaceful and homogeneously happy as it may seem at first glance (and we will show this), the image of Yugoslavia as a peaceful period of economic growth was fixed due to the atrocities, the phenomenally insane cruelty, and the cynicism that the wars of the 1990s brought to the ex-Yugoslav countries.

1945–1950s

Yugoslavia was built on the concept of "brotherhood and unity." The slogan was adapted from the Sokol gymnastic movement, which was created under Austro-Hungarian rule (Luthar and Pusnik 2010, 5).

Malcolm points out that before the Stalin-Tito rift, "Tito's policies were modeled on those of Stalin" (Malcolm 1996, 194). Only after the rift did Tito have to reorder his image into one more anti-Stalinist and liberal minded. Previously, the close ties with the Soviet Union had been visible through the official speeches of the new leaders. Furthermore, the vector of orientation can be seen through cultural patterns. For example, Soviet fashion aesthetics were highly valued in postwar Croatia. This was visible at the Zagreb Fair held in 1947. Immediately after the Stalin-Tito rift, fashion was forced to move closer to the styles of the Western world (Bartlett 2010, 408).

In the political field, two important decisions were made concerning the redefinition of the status of Kosovo and the construction of the Macedonian identity, which should be mentioned here. While the basic structure of the federation was agreed on in 1943, the status of Kosovo was undefined for more than two years. On September 3, 1945, it was declared that the Autonomous Region of Kosovo-Metohija be set as a "constituent part" of Serbia (Malcolm 1998, 315–316). For Macedonia, also having an Albanian minority and being located on the Bulgarian border, another form of identification was prepared. Since the early postwar period, communists were engineering Macedonian distinctions (in contrast to Bulgarian) in order to create an independent national identity for it. On May 3, 1945, a commission for Language and Orthography finished a new alphabet and orthography and fashioned a Macedonian language that was based on Serbian and Bulgarian (Ramet 2006, 165). The construction of nations and borders is a feature that influenced the development of the region for the following generations. However, the Albanian minority of Macedonia was forced to accept the new identity and was largely isolated from the Hoxhaist Albania (Phillips 2004, 43).

Repressions

The redistribution of power in postwar Yugoslavia cannot be understood without taking into account the main belligerents of the war: Partisans, Chetniks, and Ustashe. Furthermore, the appeal to the World War II period and the usage of ideological national narratives after the war period were actualized once again on the eve of the Balkan wars of the 1990s.

During World War II, the Ustashe government of Ante Pavelic in Croatia were following a fascist ideology of persecution of Serbs, Jews, Gypsies, and communists (Bartlett 2003, 21). "Some Jews were allowed to buy 'honorary' Aryan status and many fled the country in that way. Orthodox Serbs were also allowed to save their lives by converting to Catholicism, but many were murdered or sent to the concentration camps, the most infamous of which was at Jasenovac, on the Croatian-Bosnian border" (Ibid., 21). The number of victims of the Pavelic regime is disputed; it varies from 600,000 Serbs, Jews, Gypsies, and communists to the mere 60,000 asserted by revisionists, such as Franjo Tudjman (Ibid., 22).

Another group, the Serbian monarchist Chetniks led by Draza Mihailovic, was fighting against the Ustashe; each considered the other to be their primary enemy. The third influential group were the Partisans. Some authors state that contacts existed between the Chetniks and the Partisans, specifically between Tito and Draza Mihailovic (Matonin 2012). Such acts of collaboration were possible at the beginning of the war when Great Britain supported the Chetniks and saw Draza Mihailovic as the possible leader of the recreated Kingdom of Yugoslav (Matonin 2012); therefore, it was financially helping Chetniks. Later, their help was expanded to Tito and the Partisans, as the force gained the leading position.

After the emergence of socialist Yugoslavia, Draza Mihailovic and other Chetniks were forced to trial and executed in July 1946. The following year, Croatian archbishop Aloysius Stepinac was put on trial. The official reasons for his imprisonment for 16 years of hard labor was his collaboration with the Ustasha regime; unofficially, it was his criticism of Communist legislation and press censorship, and his refusal to break ties with the Vatican in order to establish an "independent" Catholic Church. His imprisonment was turned into house arrest in 1951 (Ramet 2006, 167). The trials of Catholic priests were ongoing. According to Vatican sources, around 300 Catholic priests were imprisoned and awaiting trial as of September 1950 (Ramet 2006, 197). Unlike Draza Mihailovic, Ante Pavelic escaped and was living in Argentina.

Hupchick estimates the number of executed forces in postwar Yugoslavia as between 30,000 and 200,000. Another author thinks up to 250,000 people were killed during the period of 1945–46 (Malcolm 1996, 194). Among those killed were Chetniks, Slovenian Home Guards, Croatian Home

Guards, and German Volksdeutsche (Hupchick 2002, 373). The right to vote was granted to everybody over the age of 18, but it was a simulation of democratic elections in which the options to choose were minimized to one party; Croatian Communists who opposed centralizing policies were arrested, and all important industries were nationalized by the end of 1946 (Hupchick 2002, 374).

In Slovenia, mass murders by the Communists were committed against Slovenian Home Guards (*domobranci*). Toward the end of the war, around 12,000 self-defense squads were retreating to Austrian territory, but very soon Great Britain extradited them back to the Partisans, who then slaughtered them (Norkus 2012, 284). One popular interpretation is to consider Tito's speech made in Ljubljana as a signal to act. The speech starts with the sentence: "The greater part of the traitors … would no longer behold our beautiful mountains and blooming fields" (Luthar 2013, 446). The Museum of Contemporary History in Ljubljana is using this interpretation of Tito's speech when representing the postwar period.

Another group of people, who are rarely mentioned when talking about the postwar period, are refugees. For instance, 15,000 civilians emigrated from Slovenia alone in the postwar era. The majority left to South and North America and Australia (Luthar 2013, 446).

Another fact was the reaction of Great Britain, which sent more than 18,000 anti-Partisan forces back to Yugoslavia at Tito's insistence; most were massacred within hours of their arrival on Yugoslav soil (Malcolm 1996, 193). Some prisoners of war were used as a prison labor force for the constructions of roads. The Belgrade-Zagreb highway was constructed by them (Malcolm 1996, 194).

Volunteer youth brigades or the so-called working brigades was one more group, who contributed to building of roads and highways in Yugoslavia. They have participated in the political and ideological enterprises that were designed to construct "brotherhood and unity." One such project was the construction of the Brcko-Banovici railway in northern Bosnia. It is interestingthat there were also foreign citizens who participated in the construction. One such foreigner was E. P. Thompson, who later became a renowned left-wing British historian (Luthar 2013, 460).

Soviet methods of governance were implemented to combat political opponents. The most famous such case was Milovan Djilas, who was criticized in the January plenum of 1954 and then imprisoned. Moreover, 23 party members were expelled from the party in connection to him, and another 20 were disciplined (Ramet 2006, 194). Sabrina Ramet points out that the period of Djilas case was one of widespread discontent and disorder among the peasants who had been forced to collectivize. They were resisting with different surreptitious methods, including smuggling and arson. In several cases, local Communists were murdered or injured. The resistance of peasants was spreading and involved, among others, discontented veterans in the northwestern Bosnian region of Cazin in May 1950. People severed telephone lines and disarmed local police. The ringleaders were immediately arrested by the authorities, but the fight had some effect: "half a million peasant households had been brought into the cooperative farm system by June 1951 but 2.5 million households remained outside the collectivist system" (Ramet 2006, 196).

The creation of the new state in the postwar period brought radically new social and cultural characteristics. First, there were crucial changes in the middle class and the elite of the prewar and of postwar eras. "The new communist elites were on average around their thirties, without formal secondary education, from rural origin" (Bartlett 2010, 413). Their program was representing the interests of peasants. "All Balkan Communist regimes leaned heavily on peasant support, and programs addressing peasant grievances were their first priority once they took power" (Hupchick 2002, 377). Hupchick emphasizes that the Communists were concentrating on the presentation of peasants' interests but not on those of city folk (Ibid.).

The new postwar situation changed several other traditional relations in the newly emerged state, in particular in gender relations and the status of youth. Both characteristics were connected with the war and the consequences it brought. Women had to assume more responsibilities and roles that had been entirely masculine in the prewar era. Many of them joined the fighters and resistance movements. "During the war, gender equality became a fact throughout the Balkans before it became a law"

(Hupchick 2002, 377). The other characteristics of the newly emerged relations were the changed status of young people, who became the active actors and leaders during the war, this shifting the tradition to recognize the oldest as the wisest.

The visible features of the Stalinist period were the campaigns against religions. The pressure on the Roman Catholic Church intensified in 1953 when contacts with the Vatican were completely terminated (Luthar 2013, 448). Yugoslavia prohibited the assembly of worshippers, repressed the religious press, and attempted to settle relations between the representatives of the church while neglecting the role of the Vatican. Once again, the force of liberalization was tied with the figure of Tito, who declared at the end of 1953 that physical attacks against priests must be stopped (Luthar 2013, 449). At the outset, the policy affected the Croatian Catholic Church due to the collaboration of its clergy with the Ustashe regime.

The Orthodox Church came under less persecution: monasteries and churches were not destroyed, as happened with some Catholic institutions. However, there was political pressure and control (Malcolm 1996, 194). Islam also was suppressed: a law forbidding women from wearing the veil was issued in 1950, *mektebs* (elementary schools in which the basics of the Koran were studied) were closed down, and Dervish orders were banned two years later. "According to some reports, Muslims doing military service or working in so-called volunteer labor brigades were forced to eat pork" (Malcolm 1996, 195). Religious practices were moving into the "grey zone" (private houses).

In 1954, a new law that guaranteed freedom of religion was passed. Two years later, a program of restoring orthodox monasteries began. The late 1950s was a time of improving treatment for Muslims. The reason was unique to the era: the Muslim community began to be used as a tool in geopolitical relations. The newly formed nonaligned movement consisted of "new friend countries," the majority of which had Islam as their official religion (Malcolm 1996, 196).

The transformation of the Bosnian Muslim identification into a nationality was a process of two decades and a result of the changes of the geopolitical relations that favored the Bosniaks. The unclear identification was visible through the census. Thus, in the 1948 census, Muslim citizens of Bosnia were able to call themselves "Muslim Serbs" (72,000), "Muslim Croats" (25,000), or "Muslim, nationality undeclared" (778,000). In the next census, in 1953, the category of "Muslim, nationality undeclared" was replaced with "Yugoslav, nationality undeclared"; 891,800 people chose this answer. The census of 1961 provided the option "Muslim in the ethnic sense." The last step to establish the new nationality was the formulation provided by the constitution of 1963, where equality was stated by in preamble of "Serbs, Croats and Muslims." Since that time, Bosnian Muslims have been treated as a national grouping (Malcolm 1996, 198). It has to be mentioned that the Muslim nationality in Bosnia was created by secularized Muslims and led by Communists. There were two distinct trends that arose at the same time: secular "Muslim nationalism" and "revival of Islamic religious belief" (Malcolm 1996, 200). In 1968, Tito recognized Yugoslavia's Muslims as a nation (Morrison 2009, 117) and this process afforded the development of Islamic identity throughout Yugoslavia, both in Bosnia, Montenegro (mostly at the Sandzak region), Kosovo, and Macedonia.

Political and economic reforms

After the Tito-Stalin rift, the political and economic situation changed dramatically because of the suspension of financial aid from the Soviet Union. In postwar Yugoslavia, manufacturing was in crisis. When the border with Italy was opened in 1950, Yugoslavs started buying massive amounts of essential goods abroad (Luthar 2013, 460).

This new economic era may be associated with the Agrarian Reform of 1953, which redirected funding to heavy industry and made Yugoslavia the fastest growing economy in the world at the end of the 1950s (Luthar 2013, 461).

Since the late 1950s, "Yugoslavia was an independent and influential member of the Communist community of states, but tied definitively to neither side in the Cold War" (Hupchick 2002, 407). To strengthen its international position, Tito created the "nonaligned" bloc of states in 1955 which was comprised of "third world states," such as Egypt, India, and other countries from Asia and Africa (Hupchick 2002, 407). Perhaps the main reason for the nostalgic mood toward Yugoslavia today is the fact that the country was much more independent and a much stronger geopolitical actor than any of the ex-Yugoslav countries are today. The 1960s, which are associated with the process of transformation from the Stalinist regime to "socialism with the human face" and accompanied by economic growth, will be presented in greater detail in the next part.

1960s

Economic reforms

The main characteristics of the 1950s for Yugoslavia were primarily its economic growth and relative freedom. In the 1950s, the standard of living was low compared to the countries of the Western bloc, but the 1960s brought significant improvement to the average standards of living. Citizens were able to travel, to study, and to speak more freely than was granted in other socialist countries in the same period (Lampe 1996, 260). The economic reforms adopted in the 1950s had remarkably transformed both the labor relations with the enterprises and their economic orientation. The important product of this reform was the self-management system, which aimed to replace the command economy with a system that included both market orientation and the ability to make decisions on the level of each enterprise individually (Swain and Swain 2009). The main theorist of the model was Edvard Kardelj, former journalist and Partisan, and a close Slovenian "comrade" of Tito.

The goal of self-management was to implement more freedoms in decision making for the working class. It was expected that the decentralization of economic power would influence the responsibility of managers and their ability to come to decisions really needed for the enterprise at the moment. Theoretically, Kardelj's self-management "was a peculiar, if not utopian, form of 'conceptional syncretism' leaning towards a fusion of Marxist, Proudhonist, Blanquist, and other socialist ideas that were often mutually antagonistic and as such continuously created disparities and conflicts" (Luthar 2013, 457).

Nevertheless, there were quantifiable successes. In economic terms, 1957–61 was a time of growth, the GNP grew at an average rate of 12 percent, personal consumption rose by 10 percent per year, and agricultural output increased about 40 percent (Ramet 2006, 209). The market reforms "revealed that 600,000 industrial workers, nearly half the industrial labor force, were employed in enterprises that operated at a loss" (Ibid., 264).

The adoption of the self-management system enabled the creation of a more palatable image for the capitalist bloc, which led to security guarantees and increased Western aid over the next several decades. (Unkovski-Korica 2014, 132). Later, the Soviet invasion of Czechoslovakia, which was perceived as a threat to the security of Yugoslavia, bolstered the self-management model ever more (Ibid., 133).

As economic prosperity was growing and cultural development was associated with large cities in Slovenia, Croatia, and Serbia, the more developed federal units were becoming the preferred destinations for rural inhabitants and people from less developed parts of the federation. Mass migration from the country became another characteristic of the decade. The condition of Kosovo, the most underdeveloped part of the federation, was typical; inhabitants were experiencing economic difficulties and cultural backwardness, which led them to emigrate to "core cities." Since 1960, the economic factor was dominant for the Serbs, Montenegrins, and Albanians who left the region (Malcolm 1998, 330).

The economic situation of Bosnia was second only to Kosovo in poor economic conditions. As early as in 1961 was officially recognized as an undeveloped region for the following reasons (Malcolm 1996, 202).

1. It had the lowest rate of economic growth in 1952–68.
2. The average income was 2 percent lower than the national one in 1947 and even 38 percent below the 1967 average national income.
3. It had the highest illiteracy rate and highest number of rural inhabitants (except Kosovo).

The high level of emigration from the region was the obvious outcome of such circumstances; the largest group of migrants was those of Serbian origin moving to big cities of other regions.

What about citizens of the most developed units of the federation? Migration flows were also visible there, but the destinations were different. The Employment Service in Ljubljana states that 62,347 people left Slovenia for the "capitalist world" during the period of 1964–69. The top destination was Germany, followed by Austria. The highest number of those who went abroad were skilled workers and professionals. With regard to regions within Slovenia, the majority were from Murska Sobota and Maribor (Slovenska Kronika 1995, 319).

Constitutional changes

Yugoslavia enacted a new constitution in 1963. It was a step to political decentralization; moreover, it enshrined the right of the republics to leave Yugoslavia. From that time onward, all federal laws and acts had to be published in four official languages: Serbo-Croatian, Croato-Serbian, Slovenian, and Macedonian) (Ramet 2006, 208). The period was associated with a decentralization of decision making and the creation of the blocks of supporters or opponents for the liberalization and federalization of economic administrative mechanisms. "Centrally planned investment [had become] impossible in Yugoslavia because it was no longer possible to agree politically about such planning" (Ramet 2006, 209). The champions of decentralization and marketization were Slovenia and Croatia, which were the most successful republics in economic terms; less developed republics and Serbia were against such reforms (Ramet 2006, 210).

In the 1960s, two blocks within the single ruling party has become visible: liberal and conservative. However, it must be noted that these labels have other connotations than in the Western societies and mean rather the relatively higher level of freedoms proposed by the liberal forces compared to the conservatives. The liberalization of the 1960s was also connected with the removal by Tito of another important figure: the Yugoslav minister of interior affairs Aleksandar Rankovic, a top Serbian leader of the conservative block and a supporter of a centralized policy model of government (Pappas 2005, 193).

Since his dismissal from the post of minister in 1966, the government began to interfere less in church affairs, but the clergy had yet to become politically active; after a series of constitutional amendments, Bosnian Muslims were recognized as a nation (Pappas 2005, 194). Therefore, the removal of Rankovic was a signal of the shift of the regime toward the "liberal" orientation, which was led by Tito.

Culture

The two dichotomous processes were actively in conflict in the 1960s. From one side, the actualization of the nationalistic discourse and from the other the response to it: establishing the Yugoslav identity.

The actualization of the nationalistic identity in Slovenia, for instance, included a growing resistance to centralism, signified by the establishment of a national cultural fund in 1962, providing an evening newscast in the Slovenian language in 1968 and other forms of support to Slovenian culture (Luthar 2013, 468). On the other side, the 1961 population census listed the category of "Yugoslav" as a national identification option for the first time (Ibid.).

With regards to culture, the 1960s brought to the federation incredible freedoms in comparison to the Soviet bloc. "After 1948, the biggest historical NO to the Soviet became a YES to jazz" (Vučetić 2010, 145). The American embassy in Belgrade was able to organize concerts of Ella Fitzgerald, Dizzy Gillespie, Louis Armstrong, and other jazz musicians in the 1960s. It was a period of cultural liberalization, the acceptance of Western trends, and the modernization of everyday life. It was the time when the first (in fact the only) Museum of Contemporary Arts was built. Moreover, it was modeled after a similar museum in New York (Vučetić 2010, 146).

The Western lifestyle became available to the average Yugoslav citizen and was no longer the privilege of wealthy individuals. There was free access to different Western radio stations, including Radio Luxemburg, Radio Freedom, and the Voice of America (Vučetić 2010, 147). Knowing the latest hits became common.

By 1965, there were 88 official rock bands in Belgrade alone (Vučetić 2010, 147). However, each recording company had to have a responsible editor who was always a party member and was required to review all rock songs before an album would be pressed (Ramet 2002, 139).

Rock music was integrated into the socialist system: young rockers were able to play their songs on different official events and record their music at state companies. However, what made mainstream socialist rock different than that of the West was the lack of rebellion in their lyrics; moreover, some songs were truly integrated into the socialist model, because they were dedicated to Tito (Vučetić 2010, 149). "By sponsoring rock recordings, rock groups, opening disco clubs, organizing rock concerts, letting rock be visible through the media and through a specialized rock magazine, like Jukebox, they controlled the younger generation and enabled them to be part of the two different worlds" (Vučetić 2010, 161). The additional role of the magazine was that of representing the Western lifestyle to the socialist youth and to expand their list of their heroes from World War II soldiers to rock musicians like Mick Jagger (Ibid., 162).

Economic growth, decreasing centralization, possibilities to travel abroad, increasing standards of life, cultural freedoms, social security, and the good international image of Yugoslavia made many inhabitants loyal to the regime. "In times of economic prosperity there was a great consensus among the Yugoslavs that the 'best system' in the world was neither totalitarian communism nor an exploitative capitalist one" (Luthar and Pusnik 2010, 8).

Lampe summarizes the main elements that contributed to successful transformation of the 1960s as a "promising time" as (1996, 260–292):

1. Successfully balancing between East and West:
   1.1. Openness to the Western markets, especially Italy;
   1.2. Creation of the nonaligned movement;
   1.3. Continued connections with America;
2. The economic reform of 1965 was "the most ambitious set of market-oriented changes undertaken anywhere in the Communist world prior to 1989" (Lampe 1996, 261);
3. Giving breathing space to intellectual freedom.

These three main aspects of transformations led to the following consequences:

1. The opening of Western markets allowed skilled labor to obtain professional experience and, if they returned to Yugoslavia, they were able to develop good careers.
2. Relations with the United States and Britain allowed independence from the Soviet Union.
3. Ability to obtain credit, especially from the United States and the World Bank.
4. Rise of educational standards.
5. Urbanization of the culture via rural mass migration to large cities.
6. Use of free speech and religious practices.

1970s

The 1970s can be associated with economic stagnation and the tightening of repressive activities against the "liberal orientation" in the party and the society. Unlike the 1960s, which were characterized by a certain level of liberalization, the 1970s generally represented a return to more repressive policies. The federalization (instead of centralization) tendency, however, remained untouched since the autonomy of the republics and autonomous provinces were further increased in the 1974 Constitution.

The essential events of the decade are the emergence and suppression of two protests: the "Croatian Spring," and protests that took place in Kosovo. Many politicians and student activists were imprisoned. After the suppression, Croatia became known as a "silent republic" (Bartlett 2003, 33). Luthar and Pusnik argue that it was the time of the first ethnic tensions, which emerged together with economic difficulties. They think the first protest was a movement against Serb hegemony known as the "Croatian Spring" of 1971, which prompted the creation of a new constitution in 1974 (Luthar and Pusnik 2010, 6). Grandits (2008, 27) sees the national awakening as the result of the implementation of the self-management economy, because it increased the influence of national elites in each of their markets. In the broader political context, the national awakening or national "liberation," which was opposed to national "oppression," was part of the ideological socialist "emancipation" discourse (Grandits 2008, 21).

The second aspect of the same political shift "of the idea of a socialist Yugoslavism was finally replaced by the concept of the unity of the Yugoslav nations and nationalities." It was realized with the adoption of the constitution of 1974 (Grandits 2008, 23), which fixed the power of the party elites of the nationally defined constituent republics over the central party institutions. This led to an increase of the concentration on "their republics" and "national interests" (Grandits 2008, 24).

The roots of the Croatian Spring may be found in the long-term process of increased concern regarding "Serbanization." Croatian intelligentsia and journalists were calling attention to the Serbian threat in four ways: "the use of textbooks to suppress Croatian national sentiments, the Serbianization of the Croatian language, the demographic displacement of Croats by Serbs, and the encouragement of Dalmatian sentiment in order to split Croatia in two" (Ramet 2006, 230). Ramet emphasized that such possibilities were not intentionally planned but reflections of real tendencies (Ramet 2006, 229).

Ante Cuvalo compared Croatian textbooks and determined that there was a minimization of the word "Croatian" while the word "Serbian" occurred 30 times in one chapter. The Croatia-Serbian language was symbolically repressed by a reduction in the Croatian forms of words to the status of dialect, while the Serbian version was presented as a standard. The given example was visible when analyzing the Serbo-Croatian and Croatia-Serbian dictionary (Ramet 2006, 231).

With the general liberalization of the media discourse, Croats began to revise the past, reinterpret and actualize "lost heroes" such as Stjepan Radic, the leader of the Croatian Peasant Party, Josip Jelacic, and others. Public discussions were rife with proposals to install monuments to these men in different cities.

Noteworthy is the case of the city of Sibenik, where "swept along by euphoria" it was decided to cancel plans to erect monument dedicated to the victims of the Fascist regime and to construct instead a monument to the Croatian king, Peter Kresimir IV (Ramet 2006, 237). Another example of ideological shifts were the public conferences organized by Matica Hrvatska where the purity of the Croatian language became essential. It was claimed, for instance, that Yugoslav Railway use only Serbian version (*ekavian*) instead of Croatian (*ijekavian*); in 1971, Yugoslav Railway agreed to have all their notices, schedules, and forms to be pronounced and printed in the Croatian version as well (Ramet 2006, 238). In response, the Serbian population in Croatia was having growing concerns about their safety. Belgrade periodicals were adding fuel to the fire by publishing provocative articles, sometimes based on fabrications. Such was the case of "Podravska Slatina," when the Belgrade magazine *Politika* presented members of Matica Hrvatska as anti-Yugoslav Croatian nationalists who refused to attend the meeting with old Partisans in the town of Podravska Slatina. Several other tabloids carried the same news. In reaction to this there a special commission was organized, which concluded that the allegations were groundless (Ramet 2006, 250).

The support of the Croatian nationalist movement was growing and the leaders of Matica Hrvatska and Hrvatski tjednik began to test the boundaries of the system. In 1971, they demanded a separate Croatian currency, the relocation of the People's Navy to Split, the creation of a national Croatian bank, and national representation in the United Nations (Ramet 2006, 255). "Liberalization, decentralization, and appeasement of Croatia had only fed the Croats' ever-increasing hunger for autonomy" (Ramet 2006, 257) and, not surprisingly, such demands resulted in protests organized by students in support of the aforementioned reforms.

The twenty-first session of the Presidium of the League of Communists of Yugoslavia in 1972 condemned the growing exclusivist nationalism and called for stern measures. As a result, tens of thousands of members were expelled from the Croatian communist party, some 200–300 persons were imprisoned, and Matica Hrvatska and 14 periodical publications were shut down (Ramet 2006, 259).

Another protest and its suppression took place in Kosovo by Albanian inhabitants.

Tito visited Kosovo for the first time only in March 1967. He criticized the conditions of the Albanian population and stated that they were being rejected from factories at the time when Serbs were receiving preferences. In the same year, changes were made to the constitution of 1963, in which the autonomous province was called the "socio-political community" of Kosovo instead of "Kosmet" (Kosovo-Metohija) in Amendment XVIII. Such a term ("sociopolitical community") was used in the definition of the republic and hence, naturally, the next step would have been to grant the status of republic to the area (Malcolm 1998, 324).

In the following year, there was a demonstration in which several hundred people used the slogans "Kosovo—republic," "Down with colony politics in Kosovo" and similar for the first time. During the demonstration, one demonstrator was killed by the police, and 45 people were later given prison sentences (Malcolm 1998, 325). Nevertheless, after punishing the instigators, official Belgrade reacted in a positive way: they developed a branch of Belgrade University into the University of Pristina, where students were able to study in both Serbo-Croatian and Albanian. From 1970 to 1975, more than 200 teachers arrived from Tirana to teach the Albanian language. Malcolm thinks that roughly 30,000 students attended the university. The majority of them were Albanians; from 1968 to 1978, their number increased from 38 to 72 percent. Opening the university helped to create a class of educated Albanians; although there were more professional Albanians, the minority Serbs and Montenegrins occupied 52 percent of the managerial positions (Malcolm 1998, 327).

The growing national and ethnic conflicts, and the desire to freeze the regime in the phase of soft authoritarianism went hand in hand with stark contrasts between the more and less successful republics.

Thus, Slovenia and Croatia represented 29 percent of the population but had the majority of goods in the country, for instance, 44 percent of the newspapers and 46 percent of radio stations in 1972. Kosovo, as the most deprived, had only one Albanian-language daily newspaper and two radio stations out of 174 of Yugoslavia, and the lowest number of television owners (Ramet 2006, 269). The level of unemployment at the beginning of 1970s was also the highest in the southern republics. The lowest was in

Slovenia with 31 unemployed for every 1,000 people, 49 Croats, 73 Bosnians, 74 Vojvodinans, 77 Montenegrins, 97 Serbs, 216 Macedonians, and 310 Kosovars (Ramet 2006, 270).

Economic stagnation

Socialist self-management was failing because of its inability to harmonize two contradictory principles: market relations and centralist economy. The centralist economic relations had a tendency to implement burdensome bureaucracy that was considered necessary for "brothers-in-law and matchmakers."

In order to answer the question of why self-management did not succeed, Lampe used the example of the famous Yugoslav vehicle Zastava and its decline (Lampe 1996, 314). The enterprise was established in 1954 as a Serbian state company, which attracted $30 million in investment and trainers from Fiat in Italy. The factory had a growing demand from the domestic markets and from Eastern Europe. "Domestic and Western borrowings doubled capacity again by the end of the decade" (Ibid.). However, because of political interference, the director was pushed out in 1974. Because of the same governmental pressure, the number of employees doubled and the number of cars per worker decreased accordingly. In addition, the quality of the product worsened: delays together with serious deficiencies made only "two of every five vehicles produced … fit for sale" (Ibid.).

Culture as a political mechanism

Yugoslavia was the only socialist country taking part in the Eurovision Song competition. In 1961, a singer from Yugoslavia participated in the music content for the first time and received eighth place (Vuletic 2010, 126). Later, in the final years of Yugoslavia's existence, in 1989, it won the competition in Lausanne and received the right to host the next Eurovision competition in Zagreb (Vuletic 2010, 123).

The discussion about the need (or not) to participate in the festival arose occasionally due to the question of Yugoslavia's international image, when it did not win anything or when it was far behind the winners. However, it was useful, especially in the 1970s when the contest became one of the most popular programs in Europe, with a huge fan base who could become potential tourists to the Mediterranean Yugoslavia and the most liberal part of the socialist bloc (Vuletic 2010, 127).

1980s

The 1980s were the final decade of the Socialist Federal Republic of Yugoslavia's existence. Economic destabilization and the growth of ethical conflicts were the features of this period. The years after Tito's death or the "post-Tito era" from 1980 onward were associated with swelling hyperinflation, economic debts, ethnic tensions, and the nationalization of political ideologies (Luthar and Pusnik 2010, 8). As Hill says, "with Tito's death in 1980, the long-term clash of the country began" (Hill 2012, 276). According to Bebler (2002), the political order was characterized by the existence of eight authoritarian single party systems including two autonomous provinces (p. 130). However, the extent to which political monopoly was a widely used practice varied in each federal unit. Thus, in Slovenia, the League of Communists was most tolerant in this spectrum. Such conclusions may be illustrated by the empirical cross-country study of local officials that took place twice in the 1970s and in 1991 in Austria, Sweden, and several countries of Central and Eastern Europe. The study revealed that Slovenian elites were more democratic in their value-normative opinions than the majority of counterparts from Eastern and Central Europe and Serbia (Bebler 2002, 130).

Economic crisis

The promising economies of the 1970s were in dire straits 10 years later. It had $20 billion of debt, high levels of unemployment, and low salaries. The political and business elites in the developed countries of the federation, which for the previous two decades had been receiving greater freedom in decision making for national and regional economic development, saw less sense in maintaining the centralized political order and support of the poorest federations. The influencing factor that held back the disintegration of the system was its charismatic leader. The 1980s began with Tito's funeral and ended with the funeral of Yugoslavia. The death of the charismatic leader not only was a mental problem of a "doomsday" for millions of citizens who had lost their feelings of stability and a guaranteed future but also led to high economic debts.

Yugoslavia experienced the dismal shift from being one of the fastest growing economies to being one of most indebted countries. From a $50 million loan in 1961, the total extended by 1990 would reach almost $1 billion (Lampe 1996, 270). An additional $4 billion taken in 1961 from the World Bank brought economic development in the 1960s but had to be returned once (Lampe 1996, 270). By 1989, inflation was running at 300 percent and domestic and foreign debt was crushing; and all economic indicators were in decline (Hupchick 2002, 438). As John C. Cox puts it, "By 1988, it was hard to tell what was in worse shape, the Yugoslav polity or economy" (2005, 57). In order to confront the growing crisis, the final prime minister, Ante Marković , proposed a long-term program of economic regulations, part of which presupposed beginning the process of privatization (Cox 2005, 57).

It must be mentioned that the loans did not appear "out of nowhere" in the 1980s but were the result of the economic operations of the 1970s. The difference between the 1970s and the post-Tito period was precisely in the figure of Tito, who was a form of a "recognized guarantee" in the international arena and was able to obtain more loans even if the previous ones had not been fully paid back. The system functioned when its representative was alive; his absence signified the dissipation of the system. A continuity of government with a similarly promising leader, which enabled the functioning of the regime by similar rules, had not been created.

The economic problems were accompanied by corruption. The most prominent illustration was the scandal related to the Agrokomerc bank, which had the image of a successful business model until 1987, when it was determined that the bank was operating on $800 million of unsecured loans and was not able to pay its employees' salaries due to a lack of cash.

Additionally, it was discovered that many other banks throughout Yugoslavia were involved in the Agrokomerc debacle, as well as several members of the government (Schuman 2004, 44).

Consequently, the numbers of party members were declining over the years. In 1982, there were 2.2 million party members. It is important to mention that workers never exceeded 30 percent of the membership. The middle of the 1980s was the period of declining membership, as citizens of large cities, especially workers and students, began to leave the party. Thus, by 1989, there were a mere 1.5 million members (Lampe 1996, 336). Moreover, this decline was visible in Slovenia and Croatia since the beginning of the 1980s (Lampe 1996, 337).

By the end of the 1980s, the republics of Yugoslavia were developing in different ways, and political, cultural, and economic gaps were widening. The successful Slovenian economy was growing, and the first private factory in Yugoslavia was established near Maribor in 1986. Moreover, Slovenia established a private stock exchange in Ljubljana in 1988. The shift to private entrepreneurship became a growing trend and by 1990 there were more than 30,000 private companies in Yugoslavia (Ramet 2006, 284). In addition to the relative growth and softer communist rule, Slovenia experienced the unprecedented blossoming of different nongovernmental organizations, clubs and study circles, which seriously influenced further political choices in the 1980s (Bebler 2002, 134).

In Bosnia, in contrast, the unemployment rate was 26.7 percent in 1987; only in Kosovo was the rate higher (Ramet 2006, 271). There were differences on the level of education. Bosnia demonstrated low results: 70 percent of the population in 1971 had no more than seven years of primary school education (Ramet 2006, 271). Similar trends continued into the 1980s, making the majority of the population uncompetitive in the federal labor market.

Kosovo remained the most backward region (Ramet 2006, 274). Even though it received 48 percent from the governmental budget the Fund for the Accelerate Development of the Undeveloped Republics and Kosovo (FADURK) in 1986–90, there was little impact on regional development.

Furthermore, the economic problems were increasing because of population growth—the highest birth rate in Europe. By 1990, about 70 percent of youth were unemployed (Ramet 2006, 275).

Macedonia, which was receiving 82.9 percent of its income from light industry and had the largest sectors of its economy in metallurgy, textiles, and tobacco, was closing factories (Ramet 2006, 271). Similar things were happening in Montenegro. These factors led to the protests in Skopje (1987), Belgrade (1988), Niksic (1989), and in other cities (Ramet 2006, 283).

The growing economic crisis, the stagnation of large enterprises in the majority of the federal units, the growing unemployment together with the bureaucratic rigidity of the state officials after the death of the personality that was the guarantor of the symbolic order of the system led to the dissatisfaction with the function of the system and required new approaches to resolve the crisis. The growing discourses dealing with nationalism and requests for independence were evident throughout Yugoslavia with different levels of support among the population. However, the most radical form was in Serbia, where mass support was attracted by commonly shared ethnic identities. The actualization of the long-standing taboo of ethnic rivalries, its politicization and pragmatic manipulation with cultural symbols was becoming the dominant political narrative that would be defining the climate in the country for the next decade (Pappas 2005, 197).

Cultural transformations

The "Day of Youth" holiday, for youth all over Yugoslavia, was celebrated for the first time in 1957, when Tito renamed his birthday into it (Luthar 2013, 491). "Each year, every republic and province had its own representatives carrying the batons, which came in countless different shapes and designs .... In its 40-year history, about 20,000 relay batons had been carried across Yugoslavia" (Ibid.). It is noteworthy that the holiday continued to be celebrated after Tito's death. A good example of the transformations that had accrued in Yugoslavia in the 1980s is the example of competition that took place before the celebrations: the Youth Day Poster in 1987 in Slovenia. Many art groups submitted proposed designs and the winner was selected from among hundreds of them. A Slovenian avant-garde collective, Neue Slowenische Kunst (NSK), won the first prize. "Immediately afterwards the public found out that the poster had actually been based on a painting 'The Third Reich' by a German painter, Richard Klein" (Ibid., 489). This accident (the acceptance of the poster) showed the ideological and aesthetic similarities of both regimes. It was the last year that Youth Day was celebrated (Ibid., 490).

The NSK was formed at the beginning of 1980. Marina Grzinic argues that "[the] NSK project revealed a new cultural context and contributed to the rapid disintegration of the aesthetics and ethical standards of communist culture and identity" (Grzinic in Djurić and Suvaković 2003, 248). It consisted of three main entities, and used manifestos, performances, public provocations and intervention in politics: the music group/rock band Laibach, the visual arts group Irwin, and the "retro-grade" Scipion Nasice Theatre.

New art brings new ways of representations and new sociopolitical critiques, which is usually not supported by the existing government. The levels of nonsupport could vary from total prohibition as in the Soviet Union (e.g., the "Bulldozer Exhibition" of 1974) to the more liberal forms, as condemnation and critiques through the supporting sources of media. The response to NSK and Laibach was rather harsh: their performances were banned from 1983 to 1987.

From 1987 onward, the regime was changing dramatically, and Laibach would be a good example of the visualization of such changes. It was the most popular group in Yugoslavia and the only one that had concert tours in America. Since 1989, the band has performed in New York, Washington, Boston, and Los Angeles. It "clearly benefitted from the relatively more liberal atmosphere prevailing in Slovenia" (Ramet 2002, 138). In the other countries of Yugoslavia, it was mostly always banned. In 1989, Laibach visited and performed in Bosnia and Herzegovina for the first time. In order to see the difference between the political atmosphere of Slovenia and Bosnia, it should be noted that this visit was made under the personal responsibility of the manager of the Sarajevo's Center for the Social Activities of Youth.

What exactly was new about Laibach? They used Nazi ideology to reactualize it and to impose it on the Yugoslavian political regime. By imitating the Nazi aesthetics, they wanted to oppose or to demonstrate the similarities with the politics of their time, but in such way were doubly oppressed by the state: as "Nazi-sympathizers" and as the critics of the Yugoslav regime (Djurić and Suvaković 2003, 252–253).

Another characteristic of the cultural life of the 1980s was the actualization of national interests through a culture that was visible throughout Yugoslavia and was reflected though the popular media, ideas, and culture. The political ideas were represented through the alternative culture with happenings and avant-garde music. The most famous were Neue Slowenische Kunst with its Laibach, Novi Evropski Poredak (New European Order) from Zagreb, Autopsije in Ruma, Aporea (Apokrifalna Realnost) (Apocryphal Reality) from Skopje, and Metropolie Trans from Osijek. They were not juxtaposed because they appealed to the different historical epochs, which were not the same for each country (Ramet 2002, 38). Neue Slowenische Kunst was using a pseudo-Nazi ideology, Macedonian Aporea-Byzantium, which was relevant only for it. A unique band from Macedonia "Aporea" had produced one album in 1988; it was then transformed into group "Anastasia." The empire was called "Byzantine rock" (for lack of a better term); it contained orthodox liturgical music in a rock format.

The 1980s brought new forms of displaying reality: alternative music and art and an actualized search of national roots. Byzantine or Monarchic, punk or post-gothic, it was a new form of reflection about the individual and the polity, which could not be implemented before.

Another form of supporting democratic values was the Slovenian magazine *Mladina* (Youth), which became famous in the 1980s and remains an independent political journal for youth. It went through different decades of existence from 1943, being under party control until receiving its independence on publishing "avant-garde oppositional weekly" in the 1980s (Cox 2005, 62). It was the source of alternative analysis not only for Slovenians who bought 65,000 copies per week but also for other former Yugoslav audiences (Cox 2005, 62). *Mladina* and the monthly *Nova Revija* became an influential embodiment of civil society that accumulated intellectuals, journalists, political activists, and dissidents (Bebler 2002, 135)

Growing nationalism

In the early 1980s, historical revisionism became the dominant discourse among Serbian historians. Ramet states that the revisionism became a visible tendency in Serbia in 1977 when a novelist Dobrica Cosic claimed that Serbs were exploited by all other Yugoslav nations.After Tito's death, the point was legitimized by various publications (not only by Serbian novelists but also by historians), who claimed similar ideas. The nodal point of fixing the national problem perhaps appeared with publishing the extracts of a "memorandum" by the Academy of Science and Art on September 25, 1986. It was signed by 200 scholars who claimed that Tito's policy had aimed at the weakening of Serbia (Malcolm 1996, 206). "The memorandum portrayed the Serbs as the great victims of Tito and Communist rule and accused Croats and Albanians ... of alleged 'genocidal' policies against ethnic Serbs" (Ramet 2002, 20). The additional push to the publishing of the memorandum was the trial of ex-Nazi Andrija Artukovic in Zagreb in September 1986, who was charged with "ordering and causing" the death of 231,000 men in Yugoslavia during World War II (Ramet 2002, 21). The revision of history was gaining momentum. The emergences of two new burning issues: the imprisonment practices of Goli Otok and other prisons, together with the reassessment of the period of World War II from the standpoint of national suffering (Ibid., 154).

It can be seen that 1980 was a turning point for broad revisions of the past with developing new frames: those of national historical interpretations. The broad varieties of novels, memorials published since 1980 in Serbia shifted to the rhetoric of victimization of the Serbian society. This ideological shift together with public activities of the Milosevic team brought public on the streets "clamoring for their messiah to take charge of Kosovo, of Vojvodina, of Montenegro" in 1988 (Ramet 2002, 157). The politization of the history influenced everyday practices. Thus, for instance, the shelves of the bookstores were full of books reflecting the role of Kosovo in Serbian history, even a new perfume was produced with the name "Miss 1389," which is the date of the Battle of Kosovo (Ramet 2002, 37).

Following this came a wave of nationalistic sentiments made by both Serbs and Croats regarding historical revision of the territories in Bosnia. However, Malcolm points out that the growth of Serbian nationalism was more destructive, even though they should have been the most satisfied ethnic groups of all Yugoslavs because Belgrade was the place of governance, and Serbs dominated the communist party and the armed forces (Malcolm 1996, 204).

Contemporary Serbia

Describing the contemporary political, economic, and cultural situation in Serbia, experts give quite a dark evaluation. Thus, in 2005, Washington's Heritage Foundation ranked the country near the bottom of the economic freedom index. Additionally, Serbia is characterized by high levels of corruption and is a transit country for the trafficking of illegal drugs, centered in the Sandzak region (Ramet 2011, 8). Many companies and entire industries remain monopolized, such as the oil industry and Serbian Telekom, which are monopolized by the state, which is "the generator of corruption" (Ibid., 9). In 2007, Transparency International ranked Serbia below Mauritania, Malagasy, Lesotho, Burkina Faso, Ghana, and Botswana in its corruption perception index (Ibid., 9). Another alarming phenomenon, cited by the Helsinki Committee For Human Rights, is the different types of violence in all spheres of public life, such as street, domestic, and institutional violence (Dulić 2011, 28). This is accompanied by retrograde ideologies and open homophobia (Ibid., 28).

Even though the preconditions for the overall neglect of the civic values and nationalist patterns may be found in habits and culture, Ramet puts the main "success" in the activation of nationalist rhetoric on the Serbian elites, who used the special strategies and tactics of over the past quarter of a century (Ramet 2011, 10). Dulić (2011) holds a highly similar opinion, claiming that Serbia's transition has been elite-driven and did not change even after the death of Milosevic.

Dulić (2011) calls Serbia a country of "in-between Europe" (Zwischeneuropa), characterized by parochialism and the uncompleted process of nation-building (Dulić 2011, 21). It was usually balancing between two controversial narratives: Western European narratives of modernization and specifically Serbian narratives that rely on native discourses of Serbian exceptionalism (Ibid., 25). The latter is grounded in an ideological matrix of "national populism, pan-Slavic ideological trends, anti-Westernism, communism, and the weakness of civic democratic tradition in contemporary Serbia" (Ibid., 25). Dulić asserts that Serbia has a clash between parochial nationalism and Europeanism, which is typical for the nineteenth-century world of nationalism. "The very fact that Serbia has been unable to dissociate itself from its past has been responsible for Serbia's slow pace in tackling the more visible problems of weak institutions" (Ibid., 26). The cultural patterns and moral value system is still characterized by the pre-modern legacy: "provincial mindset, radical populism, traditional gender roles, clericalization, crumbled, and apathetic public" (Ibid., 30). The dominant discourse of post-Milosevic Serbia has retained the nationalist mythical frame of the narrative of a Serbian nation, introduced in the late 1980s. Paradoxically, "Slobodan Milosevic was judged and condemned only as a communist, while the nationalist essence of his ideology was never mentioned" (Stojanović 2011, 232).

In order to understand the political situation in Serbia, we would like to present the description made by Ramet, who identified four groups of citizens on the basis of their political attitudes: hard liberals, soft liberals, ultranationalists or "anti-Westerners", and the apolitical (2011, 3–8). The given description shows the broad characteristics of political division, media-orientation, and political patterns of contemporary Serbia.

Hard liberals – this group is associated with civic values, equality and tolerance. These are different scholars and activists, such as the Women in Black, the Belgrade Circle, or the Independent Society of Journalists of Vojvodina. "The most important liberal organ is *Republika*, a glossy magazine of social and political analysis" and the daily newspaper *Borba*. "The leading liberal politician in the early post-Milosevic period was Zoran

Dindic (1952–2003), who served as Prime Minister from January 2001 until March 2003, when he was gunned down on the streets of Belgrade" (Ramet 2011, 4). Today, the representative of these values is Cedomir Jovanovic.

The second group is **soft liberals** or as Ramet put it "flexible realists." The politicians from this group try to avoid dogmatism, although they may simultaneously use "nationalistic statements in an effort to woo voters not prepared [to accept] this group" (Ramet 2011, 4). From one side they use the EU integration, and, if possible, also NATO as the part of their program, from the other side the issue of Kosovo becomes the trigger. The representative of the given strategy is the politics of Boris Tadic and his DS Party and Ivica Dacic, the head of the Socialist Party of Serbia. The media representative is Danas and B-92 Radio; the scientific organ is the Institute for Contemporary Serbian History.

Ultranationalists or "anti-Westerners," the third group is characterized "by their systematic efforts to represent Serbs, indicted by the ICTY, as Serbian heroes" (Ramet 2011, 4), with claims to make closer ties with Russia, with anti-European rhetoric, with an unrelenting desire to annex the Republika Srpska and refusal to accept Kosovo's independence and with extreme homophobia and intolerance. The political representatives are the Serbian Radical Party (SRS) led until 2008 by Tomislav Nikolic, Democratic Party of Serbia, led by Vojislav Kostunica. The media-supporter is the weekly magazine *NIN*, daily newspapers *Vecernje novosti*, and *Glas javnost*, and some of the texts from *Kurir*, *Pravda*, *Tabloid*, and *Politika*. The quasi-academic journal *Nova srpska politicka misao* may be mentioned. The broad variety of ultranationalist NGO should be mentioned as well: far-right clerico-fascist organization Obraz (Honour), Nomokanon, Srpski sabor Dveri, Nacionalni stroj, Krv i cast (Blood and Honor), Pokret 1389 (the 1389 movement), Novi Srpski program, Nasi, Mlada Bosna, Familija srpskih navijaca, and Rasonalisti.

From the academic circles, some scholars from the Serbian Academy of Sciences and Art may be mentioned. Usually, the composition of their supporters is based on some students from the secondary schools, football fans, and citizens of marginal means (Ramet 2011, 7).

Apolitical is the last group with the public low on information and dogmatic on one point: "politics is bad" (Ramet 2011, 7).

Serbian society today is highly polarized, even more so than before 2003. "This polarization was also seen in the snap parliamentary elections held in May 2008, when Boris Tadic's pro-EU coalition won 38.8% of the vote against 40.5% of the vote garnered by the ultra-nationalist coalition of Tomislav Nikolic's SRS and Vojislav Kostunca's DSS" (Ramet 2011, 7).

In order to realize the course toward entering the EU, Serbia is required to adapt the standards and its legislation, which consists of more than 80,000 pages (Ramet 2011, 7). The difficulties of entering the EU can be traced because of widespread corruption, overall unpreparedness and the other factors presented above.

Kosovo

The year 1981, when Tito died and Yugoslavia entered the post-Tito era, was marked by political and economic crisis in Kosovo, which started in Pristina University and spread soon to the other cities among a wide range of people, including workers and young people. The government responded with tanks and police; 1,200 were imprisoned, while the number killed varies from 9 demonstrators and 1 policeman, according to official data, to more than 1,000 killed, according to later research (Malcolm 1998, 335).

In March 1989, the political autonomy of Kosovo and Vojvodina was abolished; the subsequent mass demonstrations were crushed by the Serbian security forces. "All the pieces of the jigsaw were now in place" (Malcolm 1996, 212). Milosevic was centralizing power; the nationalist ideology was legitimized; the economic discontent made people desire a strong leader who would gather "the Serbs into the single political unit which could either dominate Yugoslavia or break it apart" (Malcolm 1996, 212).

Kosovo had a high birth rate among both Albanians and Serbs. The birth rate among Serbian and Albanian women was nearly the same in the early 1950s. Thirty years later, the number of children per Serbian women had decreased. According to the 1981 census, Serbian women living in Kosovo had an average of 3.4 children, while Serbian women in Serbia had 1.9.

The birth rate of Albanian women from the same region averaged 6.7 children, while urban Albanian women had 2.7 children. The traditionally agricultural, rural society was the reason for the high birth rate among both Albanians and Serbians (Malcolm 1996, 332). Urbanization and modern lifestyles weakened traditional norms. Thus, there was a high birth rate among both groups in comparison to other regions but with a greater decrease of the birth rate among the Serbian population in Kosovo.

There are two main reasons given for the changes:

1. The Serbian population was urbanizing at a greater rate than the Albanian one, which caused more rapid processes in social change.
2. Serbian women had a very high level of abortion. By 1994, they had the highest abortion rate in the whole of Europe (Malcolm 1996, 333).

The 1980s saw a publishing boom, in which different Serbian authors highlighted topics of Serbian roots, the victimized Serbian character and other roots of the nation in the Kosovo area; prominent authors included Dimitrij Bogdanovic, Radovan Samardzic, and Dusan Batkovic (Malcolm 1998, 338). Serbian media were exploiting various conflicts or crimes committed by Kosovars toward Serbs as a way of discrediting the entire Albanian population of Kosovo. One such example was "The Martinovic Case," when a Serbian farmer was hospitalized in the Pristina hospital because of the forceful insertion of a glass bottle in his anus. He claimed that it was made by masked Albanians; another explanation was that the accident was a mishap during an act of self-gratification. The case became so well known that there were several commissions both in Belgrade and Kosovo to answer the question. The following year, a Belgrade journalist sold 50,000 copies of a book in the case (Malcolm 1998, 338).

As nationalist sentiments were gaining strength, the next step was the birth of a populist leader. Slobodan Milosevic exploited this trend and began to produce classic hate speeches with the themes that the safety of the entire population was decreasing; hatred and fear were becoming common. Albanians were allegedly infringing upon their rights: in March 1990, according to the "Yugoslav Program of Measures to be taken in Kosovo," a wide range of measures to strength positions of Serbs such as "new investments in Serb-majority areas, building new houses for Serbs who returned to Kosovo, encouraging Albanians to seek work in other parts of Yugoslavia, introducing family planning for Albanians ... suppressing of the Albanian-language newspaper Rilindja, the closing of the Kosovo Academy of Arts and Sciences and dismissal of many thousands of state employees" (Malcolm 1998, 346). In response, Albanians ignored the introduction of the new laws, and created parallel existing political structures. In 1992, they held a referendum in which private houses were used as polling stations and declared the independence. It was not recognized by local authorities and many Albanians were dismissed from work (Malcolm 1998, 349).

Several political movements were established, one of which found broad support: the Democratic League of Kosovo (LDK in the Albanian language), led by Dr. Ibrahim Rugova, a specialist in literary history and aesthetics. His main methods were nonviolent resistance, a boycott of Serbian laws, and the actualization of the Kosovo problem on the international level, different negotiations and petitions to the international organizations, such as the United Nations or the European Parliament (Malcolm 1998, 348). In response, Serbian policies became even harsher. Albanian doctors and teachers were dismissed (e.g., 6,000 teachers in 1990). Albanian children had to use separate classrooms and lavatories. Death from disease increased, with the decline in the number of Albanians receiving vaccinations (Malcolm 1996, 349). Albanians organized parallel school and health systems financed privately on a voluntary basis, mainly through the LDK. Arrest have become a routine. For example, in 1994, 15,000 people had "informative talks" when the police entered any Albanian house to check if the inhabitants were insulting the "patriotic feelings" of Serbian citizens" (Malcolm 1998, 348). After such conversations, police had a right to arrest people and detain them for three days. The subsequent transformation of the situation with military intervention and ethnic cleansing has made the region a black point on the European map.

After the military intervention of NATO, which was subject to numerous critiques and post-conflict settlement, Kosovo had its first elections in November 2001; Ibrahim Rugova was elected as the president and Bajram

Rexhepi as the prime minister. In the 2004 presidential elections, Rugova remained president, and the next elections made Fatmir Sejdui the new president. Since 2007, the prime minister has been Hashim Thaçi.

Kosovo declared its independence on February 17, 2008, and in the following days a number of countries recognized its independence. By 2014, 108 countries had done so, including all neighboring states except Serbia.

For protection, the United Nations established a civilian mission (UNMIK) to help with the administrating and rebuilding of the country in June 1999. Within weeks, more than 800,000 refugees returned to the country (Mehmeti 2013, 187). UN Secretary-General Kofi Annan oversaw the organization of the four-pillar structure of UNMIK, in which the EU had to deal with economic reconstruction, and the OSCE was entrusted with the task of institution building and promoting democracy. However, the intent to help has created a country that is mostly controlled by the UN presence (Mehmeti 2013, 197). Local politicians have only limited responsibilities, while the real power remains with the Special Representative of the secretary general (Mehmeti 2013, 197).

The presence of international institutions contributed to democratic development, but the problems of corruption, money laundering, and organized crime remain (Mehmeti 2013, 201).

Slovenia

As all other countries of the Yugoslavian bloc did, Slovenia left communism under conditions of extreme macroeconomic instability and hyperinflation (Norkus 2012, 274). Because of already-established economic relations with the Western European business markets (25 percent of Slovenian external economic relations at the end of the 1980s were with capitalist countries [Feldmann 2006: 843]), Slovenian companies had relatively rapidly and successfully adjusted to the new economic conditions and switched from a centrally planned economy to a market-oriented economy (Tomsic and Prijon 2013, 79). Such an impressive rapid adaptation was possible due to a number of different factors, such as long exposure to the West, high educational levels, relatively efficient civil services, the highest GNP in the communist world, and other aspects (Bebler 2002,

131). The geographic location and higher homogeneity of the population in terms of ethnicity and religious identification contributed positively to the challenging transformations (Cabada 2008, 30; Bebler 2002, 131).

The overall rapid reorganization of business strategy toward the Western market affected the former Yugoslavia market relations. Thus, in 1992, sales to the former Yugoslavian republics fell from US$ 6.7 billion to only US$ 1.5 billion (Damijan 2004, 273).

The political transformations were atypical. Slovenia had two influential former communist political parties instead of one; moreover, they were competing with the third and most influential ex-communist party (the "mother" of the communist union) (Norkus 2012, 275). One of them was the Party of Liberal Democracy of Slovenia. It was descended from the Slovenian "Comsomol," which means the Young Communist League of Slovenia and the United List of Social Democrats (Norkus 2012, 275). Another exceptional feature of Slovenia's post-communism transformation was the new political practice of frequently organizing referendums. In the early 1990s, Slovenia could be compared only to Switzerland in this regard (Norkus 2012, 281).

Slovenia and Croatia were the first Yugoslav republics to declare their independence. Previously, in April 1990, the first multiparty elections had taken place in Slovenia. The parliamentary elections resulted in a win of the Democratic Opposition of Slovenia (DEMOS); with 54 percent of the vote, it dominated the main house of the tricameral Republic Assembly (Bebler 2002, 132). DEMOS was a coalition of center-right political parties that emerged at the end of 1989. It included the Slovenian Democratic Union, the Slovene Christian Democrats, the Social Democrat Alliance of Slovenia, the Farmers' Alliance, and the Greens of Slovenia (Ibid.). The leader of the DEMOS coalition was Joze Pucnik, a Slovenian dissident.

In contrast to the parliamentary results, the results of presidential elections on April 8 brought to the victory the candidate of the reformed communist party, who had led the communists in Slovenia from 1986, Milan Kucan (Crampton 2002, 455). He defeated the candidate from DEMOS and became the first freely elected president (Ibid.). The first government was headed by Lojze Peterle, leader of the Christian Democrat Party. The former communist party together with their youth wing, called the Liberal Democrats, and the Socialists became the opposition.

The ethnic composition of Slovenia consisted of the Slovenian majority (88 percent), 8 percent were Croats, followed by only 2.4 percent of Serbs, and 1.6 percent Hungarians and Italians (Nigel 2006, 12). The total population was 1,966,000 people.

A year later, on June 26, 1991, Slovenia declared independence from Yugoslavia. As Hupchick observed, "the Communist era ended everywhere in the Balkans by the close of 1991" (2002, 441). The following day, the Yugoslav Army (JNA) attacked.

After the attempts of the JNA to reestablish control under the territory of Slovenia (the period of the Ten-Day War) and after other legislative procedures, the presidents of the SFRJ, Slovenia and European Union met on Veli Brijun where they signed the Brijuni Declaration. On October 26, the last JNA troops left the country. According to Nigel (2006, 20), Slovenes had suffered 19 dead and 192 wounded, also 12 foreigners, who were crews of commandeered lorries were killed during JNA air raids. Slovenia was recognized as an independent country first by the Vatican, the neighboring country of Croatia, and the Baltic countries, followed by the EU. It became a full member of the United Nations on May 22, 1992. Slovenia became the first ex-Yugoslav state to join NATO (March 29, 2004) and the European Union on May 1, 2004.

In the economic sector, visible state regulations and monopolies have remained. Thus, after the year 2000, there were limited foreign direct investments. The explanation is based on the concept of the "ideology of national interest" (Tomsic and Prijon 2013, 77). The majority of the banking sector is still owned by the state.

The political sector was characterized by a bipolar division into two political blocks: "leftist" and "rightist" or "old" and "new" (Adam and Tomšič 2012, 80). The first block was represented by the Liberal Democracy of Slovenia (LDS) and the Social Democrats (SD), the successors to the former ruling Communist Party. Three main "new" parties appeared: the Slovenian Democratic Party (SDS), the Slovenian People's Party (SLS), and New

Slovenia (NSi) (Ibid.). The LDS remains an important political player today. Another party, called Positive Slovenia (PS), led by the mayor of Ljubljana Zoran Jankovic, was established in 2011 and won the parliamentary elections the same year. However, it did not manage to form a coalition in parliament. Therefore, at the beginning of 2012, a center-right government coalition was formed (Ibid., 97). It was led by the leader of the SDS, Janez Jansa but, due to a corruption scandal, three of five coalition parties left the coalition and the new coalition based on center-leftists established a new government. It was led by Alenka Bratusek from PS (Ibid., 97). In the 2014 parliamentary election, the newly established party "Party of Miro Cerar" (SMC) won. The second and third parties were the Positive Slovenia and Democratic Party of Pensioners of Slovenia (DeSUS).

Voting activity has been decreasing over the years and corresponds to the decreasing trust in political institutions (Makarovič and Tomšič 2010). Through most of the years of the transformation period, both political and economic life in Slovenia have been characterized by a "cultural hegemony that was undertaken by a 'leftist' camp" (Adam and Tomšič 2012). This means that the ideas, values or solution that were proclaimed by left-oriented actors "received much more media attention and support from opinion-makers" (Ibid., 86). Such tendencies remain today.

Croatia

The first party to be established in early 1989 was the Croatian Social Liberal Party (Hrvatska Socijalno-Liberalna Stranka [HSLS]) set up by Drazen Budisa and other non-Communist liberal intellectuals from Zagreb. The leader was a former student activist of 1971, who had been imprisoned at that time. It was a centrist party that attracted educated voters. "In early 1989 they organized a petition to restore the monument of the Croatian national hero Ban Jelacic, which had been removed from the main square in Zagreb in 1945" (Bartlett 2003, 34). It was signed by 70,000 people, and such a large number was an unprecedented phenomenon was a sign of the entry of political pluralism, thinks Bartlett (Ibid.).

In June 1989, the Croatian Democratic Union was established by Franjo Tudjman, a former general in the Partisan army in the World War II and later a nationalist activist of Croatian Spring. "In the program of 'national reconciliation' the privileged position of Serbs in the upper echelon of power was to be swept away" (Bartlett 2003, 34). His support was the Croatian diaspora from Canada and the United States. One of Tudjman's supporters was Gojko Susak, Croatian emigrant from Canada, who later became the defense minister.

Franjo Tudjman was elected president of the republic and a new constitution with the national focus was introduced in December 1990. "A new Citizenship Law was also passed. It allowed ethnic Croats who lived abroad the right to apply for Croatian citizenship. The law permitted a large number of ethnic Croats living in the Herzegovina region of Bosnia to become Croatian citizens and thus to vote in Croatian elections" (Bartlett 2003, 34). In contrast, nonethnic Croats had to apply for citizenship, wait for five years and pass a citizenship exam of the Croatian language (Ibid., 36). Serbians' statuses were changed from "constituent nation" to "national minority." The politics of new government from one side and Belgrade-based anti-Croatian press propaganda increased the tensions between the two groups in mixed communities (Ibid., 37).

On the official level, Croatia was moving toward stronger decentralization. Municipalities and cities became the two new lowest levels of self-governing units. However, the authoritarian tendencies of Tudjman with significant interference into the affairs of counties and inappropriate settings of financial standards limited their freedom in decision making (Cabada 2008, 29).

A referendum on independence was held on May 19, 1991; 93 percent voted for independence.

The HDZ began to have authoritarian tendencies in 1995; for instance, in November 1996, the government attempted to close down the popular independent radio station, Radio 101. A mass protest was attended by over 100,000 people in Zagreb. Tudjman rode out the protest, much as Milosevic did, but his popularity was seriously damaged and diminished over the next several years. Similar protests took place in Belgrade in 1996-7 and were also oppressed there (Bartlett 2003, 50). Bartlett continues:

"[Tudjman's] popularity remained undiminished despite his obvious authoritarian tendencies and he succeeded in winning presidential elections in June 1997 with a 61 percent share of the vote" (Bartlett 2003, 51).

The HDZ controlled the media. The main newspaper distribution company, Tisak, had a virtual monopoly on the circulation of the printed media, controlling 65 percent of the newspaper and magazine distribution market. Opposition journals had little chance of being widely distributed, or had long delays for being paid (Bartlett 2003, 53).

Croatia declared its independence at the same time as Slovenia, but its border with Serbia, together with a 12 percent Serbian minority living in Croatia, made the intention to disintegrate peacefully and to become independent baffling.

A self-proclaimed Serb state "The Republic of Serbian Krajina" (RSK), which was organized within the territory of the Republic of Croatia and existed formally from 1991 until 1995, was economically and politically dependent upon Serbia. Later, when brought to the International Criminal Tribunal for the former Yugoslavia (ICTY), the former president of RSK, Milan Babic, stated that the separatist enclave was receiving weapons from the Milosevic government (Armatta 2010, 161). In combination with the ethnic cleansing committed in Vukovar, Hill (2012) considers the Serbian force to be the aggressors of the war (p. 277).

"Under the leadership of late Croatian President Franjo Tudjman's political party, the communist interpretation of WWII started to be questioned. The new historical paradigm went in the direction of relativization of the Croatian fascist past" (Cvijic 2008, 716). In a history textbook of 1998, the crimes of the Ustasha were mentioned, but more space is devoted to a description of the crimes committed by the Partisans, accounting for a quarter of the book. The book also contains an entire page dedicated to Partisan crimes against Croats in Bleiburg, which Cvijic (2008, 721) sees as a strategy of diverting attention. However, after the "Tudjman era," the strategy of omission that prevailed in the 1990s changed to a more accurate accounting of the crimes committed by the NHD (Cvijic 2008, 718).

Cvijic (2008) showed how the Bleiburg massacre was constructed as an important place of commemoration for state politicians from Croatian

Democratic Party (Hrvatska demokratska stranka, HDS). During the same period, the historical revisionism and "Ustasha-crime denials" increased, but the author observes that such a political position became marginal after 1999 (death of Tudjman) (Cvijic 2008, 718). The contemporary politics of commemoration of the Croatian state also include regular commemorating of "the anniversary of the liberation of the Ustasa concentration camp of Jasenovac by the prisoners," and the majority of history textbooks have upgraded their interpretation of the Ustasha role (Cvijic 2008, 720).

The death of Tudjman marked the end of the old era. "For many Croatians the event was understood as the end of an era. The whole year was characterized by the new government's attempt to move away from the previous government's policy direction" (Zambelli 2010, 1161). Consequently, cooperating with the ICTY was among the top priorities in the year 2000 and was viewed as a shift from Tudjman's policy of limited cooperation back to Westernizing the country (Zambelli 2010, 1666). At the same time. the recent war was viewed in Croatia as a Homeland War, and the new government had to balance between these two dimensions or to distance itself from first option. The distancing from the old politics and recognition of the crimes was the biggest struggle. The main crimes consist of "1993–1994 war with Bosnian Muslims and in the 1995 expulsion of ethnic Serbs from Croatia through operations Flash and Storm" (Fisher 2006, 178). In 2001, the national census showed that the number of Serbs had decreased from 12.2 percent a decade earlier to 4.5 (Ibid.). Zambelli (2010) showed how two main mutually exclusive discourses ("West-EU" and "East Balkans") were constructed and served as a basis for addressing the nature of cooperating with the ICTY. These two official discourses represented how national identity was being transformed in the country. By choosing the "West-EU" direction and distancing itself from the "East Balkan" discourse, Croatia entered the EU in 2013. Croatia was the first country in the ex-Yugoslavian conflict zone to initiate a campaign to apprehend its own war criminals (Fisher 2006, 180). The cooperation with International Criminal Tribunal for the former Yugoslavia (ICTY) was not flawless, but after final delivery of general Ante Gotovina in 2005 to ICTY, the country's path to inclusion in the EU (2013) and NATO (April 2009) was clear (Ramet 2010, 275).

The transformations in Croatia have been profound and brought a systemic change "by moving from a socialist system during Yugoslavia towards a right-wing authoritarian system in the nineties, and then towards a liberal system from 2000 onwards" (Popović 2014, 194).

Bosnia and Herzegovina

In response to the growth of unemployment, nationalistic sentiments in other countries and dissatisfaction with the living conditions, Bosnia and Herzegovina followed the example of Slovenia and Croatia and organized a referendum on independence in March 1992. This event was preceded by the first multiparty elections in the country. Characteristically, three ethnic parties won: Bosniak, Serbian, and Croatian Democratic parties. They have formed a coalition government and each of the leaders received its position in the unified government. The president of the country became the leader of the Bosniak party, the president of the parliament was the Bosnian Serb and the Bosnian Croat was nominated as prime minister.

The decision on initiating the referendum on independence was boycotted by Bosnian Serbs, who left the assembly in protest. They called on the citizens of Bosnia with Serbian ethnicity to boycott the referendum. In the end, the results were predictably unambiguous: the majority of citizens wanted to live in independent countries; 98 percent of those who voted in the referendum were in favor of independence, but approximately 35 percent of eligible voters did not participate in it. The Serbian minority announced about its desire to form the Serbian Republic of Bosnia and Herzegovina. The background of the upcoming war fits into the overall picture of Yugoslavian dissolution, in which Milosevic, with the support of Serbian nationalists, were the initiators of atrocities (Hill 2012, 277–279).

Simultaneously, the Serbian Volunteer Guard, led by Vuk Draskovic, appeared. In the summer of 1992, the Bosnian-Serb general Ratko Mladic, leading the local militia, destroyed some of the most important highways in Bosnia, commandeered the Sarajevo airport, and the three-year siege of

Sarajevo started (Schuman 2004, 50). February 5, 1994, saw the collective murder of 68 civilians at an outdoor market in Sarajevo by a "Serb mortar shell" (Schuman 2004, 52). However, the worst was yet to come: in July 1995, Srebrenica, a town located close to the Serbian border, was turned into a killing field; over 7,000 Muslim civilians were murdered under the supervision of Ratko Mladic (Schuman 2004, 52).

The pattern of committing atrocities in Bosnia in 1992 "was set by young gangsters in expensive sunglasses from Serbia" (Malcolm 1996, 252). The author does not believe the claim that the country was forever seething with ethnic hatreds; watching Radio Television Serbia in 1991–92 made this clear. As Belgrade journalist Milos Vasic explained, it was as if all television in the United States had been taken over by the Ku Klux Klan, with every little station everywhere taking the same editorial line. Under such conditions, war would be inevitable anywhere (Malcolm 1996, 252).

Ramet remarks that the conflict of 1991–95 was seen by many as a return to and a continuation of World War II, with the distribution of forces to the main ideological opponents as Chetniks and Ustasha (Ramet 2002, 26). The third group on which Serbian chauvinism was worked out was the Bosnian Muslim group.

In 1991, the ethnic composition of Bosnia and Herzegovina was next: 43.77 percent Muslim, 31.46 percent Serb, and 17.34 percent Croat (Ramet 2002, 27). "Ethnic Muslims were a relatively small minority in Yugoslavia and consisted of about 9 percent of the total population in 1984" (Ibid.). In religious terms, they represented about 3.8 million people or 16 percent of the total population (Ibid., 119).

In the Sarajevo region at the end of the 1980s, there were the highest number of mosques, 1,092, and 569 medzids (smaller places of worship), followed by the Pristina region with 445 mosques and 19 medzids, Skopje with 372 mosques and 19 medzids, and the Titograd region (Montenegro) with 76 mosques and 2 medzids (Ramet 2002, 119–120).

Since the growth of nationalism, the Serbian Orthodox media supported it and published articles on the Kosovo question; they took part in broad celebrations of the Battle of Kosovo. At the same time, Muslim media did not have such leverage. As Ramet clearly indicated, Muslims were not allowed to celebrate significant dates in the Muslim world, such as the Ottoman conquest of Bosnia (Ramet 2002, 122).

With the collapse of Yugoslav socialism, Bosnians experienced not only the destruction of the country to which they belonged but the disappearance of an entire socioeconomic order (Baker 2012, 849). As a result of the Bosnian conflict and foreign intervention (according to the author), one new occupational group emerged: interpreters. Most were locals, not professional linguists, who were hired by foreign military and civilian agencies (Baker 2012, 850). This small example shows the serious transformation in the employment that came with the war. The siege of Sarajevo, Srebrenica, and other massacres had soon become part of Bosnian history.

The 1995 Dayton Peace Agreement stopped the war on the physical level, but further strengthened the ethnic segregation of the country by legitimizing the new union of the country: Republica Srpska. As a result, the contemporary country exists in a form of coexistence of the Federation of Bosnia and Herzegovina predominantly composed of Bosniaks and Croats and the Serbian unit of Republica Srpska. The political center for the first entity is Sarajevo, for the second Banja Luka. Each has its own government. The central parliament in Sarajevo is led by a tripartite presidency, which consists of a representative of each ethnic group: Bosniak, Croat, and Serb. However, Bosnia still lacks some national ministries; no common ministry of economy, of education and others exists.[8] Republica Srbska, "The post-Dayton creation" has autonomy and ambivalent relations with Serbia.

Bosnia and Herzegovina is facing tremendous economic problems with an official unemployment rate of 40 percent (or at least a 27 percent unemployment rate if the "gray" economy is counted), political instability, and high levels of corruption.[9]

8 Myr tsinoyu stahnatsiyi: rezul'tat skladnoho kompromisu v Bosniyi—urok dlya Ukrayiny (in Ukrainian), Radio Liberty, April 7, 2015, http://www.radiosvoboda.org/audio/26602644.html

9 http://www.balkaninsight.com/en/article/bosnia-elections-2014-profile

Macedonia

Macedonia played a small role in the disintegration of Yugoslavia and had hoped to bring all the republics together with new federation agreements (Rossos 2008, 261; Phillips 2004, 49). As a part of the federation, Macedonia greatly valued that status and only the aggressive invasion of the Yugoslav army in Slovenia made it clear that peaceful scenarios will not work. On one side, it benefited from its status as an autonomous republic; on the other, Yugoslavia protected it from Bulgarian and Greek political influence, territorial disputes, and Serbian dominance from the other side of the border.

While the balance between external security and inner autonomy has ceased to exist, Macedonia finished 1989 with internal political and economic reforms. Privatization reforms and the first multiparty system was initiated. At the end of the 1980s, new parties emerged, representing the interests of pro-independence sympathizers and of the Albanian and Turkish minorities. The former communists first became known as the League of Communists of Macedonia–Party for Democratic Renewal; in 1991, they changed the title to the Social Democratic Union of Macedonia (SDSM). The party presenting the Albanian interests was established as the Party for Democratic Prosperity (PDP) with its leader, an English teacher, Nevzat Halili; the Turkish minority representative was the Democratic Party of Turks (DPT). Altogether, 20 parties participated in the parliamentary elections. The presidential elections were won by Kiro Gligorov, a 74-year-old lawyer, experienced in governmental work (Rossos 2008, 264).

Later, on September 8, 1991, a referendum took place with a turnout of 72.16 percent; the majority of the voters (95.08 percent) supported independence and 3.63 percent opposed it. As Rossos (2008, 267) points out, as "a sign of internal troubles to come" the Albanian minority boycotted the referendum in order to protest "the government's non-compliance with their demands" (Phillips 2004, 51), for example, the demand to reopen the Albanian secondary schools that were recently closed.

Two weeks after the referendum, the declaration of independence was approved, and within two months (17 November) the new constitution was adopted. Finally, on the November 20, the official proclamation of independence was initiated (Rossos 2008, 266).

The new constitution defined a parliamentary government with the president as the head of the state and a national assembly (Narodno Sobranie) as a legislative power of the country. The assembly or parliament consisted of 120 members chosen by voters for four years by direct elections (Rossos 2008, 267). Gligorov, still the president, initiated the secret negotiations with Milosevic and the latter agreed to withdraw all Yugoslav army units from the territory of the Macedonian state. Macedonia was the only republic fortunate enough to withdraw from Yugoslavia and to attain independence peacefully (Rossos 2008, 267). Similar to Slovenia, Macedonia had a small community of Serbs (circa 45,000) and such circumstances, together with its economic backwardness and location, allowed Belgrade nationalists to not be concerned about the breakaway of this republic from the Greater Serbia project (Phillips 2004, 52).

However, the new established country, seeking recognition from the European Community, faced political oppression from the other side of the border: the Greek one. Greece claimed that the new republic represented a security threat and demanded changes to the constitution. Macedonia adopted the requisite changes in January 1992 and according to the Badenter Commission "fulfilled all conditions for diplomatic recognition" (Rossos 2008, 268). Nevertheless, they were met with a new list of demands, which were produced mostly for inner-Greek political consumption consisting of "the modern Greek imperialism idea" to have "exclusive ownership of all things and matters Macedonian: geography, history, traditions, symbols, and, most important, the Macedonian name itself" (Rossos 2008, 269). This was unacceptable for Macedonia because its liberation discourse was grounded in nineteenth-century romantic nationalism and based on identifying the national majority with the particular name "Macedonia and Macedonians." In such circumstances, the loss of the given name meant the confirmation of self-nonexistence as a nation for the majority of the ethnic population.

The protests in Athens and Saloniki in support of the official line of Greek politics have intensified the anti-Macedonian narrative. Thus, during the protests, the public clamored against the "counterfeit nation" and "pseudo-Macedonians" (Rossos 2008, 270). The year 1993 was associated with the 18-month embargo initiated by Greece from the south and the disruption of trade to the north caused by the Balkan wars. Such circumstances lead to economic collapse with the loss of 60 percent of the nation's trade (Rossos 2008, 270). According to the U.S. Department of State, Macedonia's GDP of 1995 has declined to 41 percent of its 1989 level as a result of border closures from both sides (Rossos 2008, 276).

Finally, after four years of negotiations, Macedonia and Greece signed the agreement in New York in 1995, in which Greece agreed to lift the embargo and recognize the country in the exchange for the new Macedonian flag without a Vergina star and forswore any claims on Greek territory (especially on Aegean Macedonia). Such agreement led to the international recognition of the Macedonia with its temporary title of FYROM by the United Nations and European countries. The reference to the country as FYROM had to be temporary, resolved as soon as Greece approved one of the suggested names, and Macedonia would also consider it as an appropriate title. However, the issue has not been resolved so far while Greeks rejected proposed titles as "Nova Macedonia" or "Upper Macedonia" and Macedonia did not prefer such options as "Vardar Republic" or "Central Balkan Republic," proposed by Albanian activists (Phillips 2004, 59).

Another difficulty appeared in the field of international recognition was the language issue. While Bulgaria was the first country to recognize Macedonia, it considered the Macedonian language and nation as being "western Bulgarian" (Phillips 2004, 59).

Regarding politics, the 1994 presidential elections were won by the former president Gligorov, resulting in an unstable political situation and a newly established opposition. The 1999 presidential elections reflected tremendous political changes and a shift from the dominant party of Social Democrats to right-wing parties with nationalist and anti-Communist positions. After the second round of elections, the president was Boris Trajkovski the leader of the VMRO-DPMNE, the Internal Macedonian Revolutionary Organization–Democratic Party of Macedonian National

Unity (Vnatresna Makedonska Revolucionerna Organizacija–Demokratska Partija za Makedonsko Nacionalno Edinstvo) (Rossos 2008, 276).

The changes in the voters' political preferences were also related to external problems. The 1999 Kosovo conflict led to the worsening of the economic situation, while the Macedonian economy was greatly dependent on imports, exports, or transition through Serbia and Montenegro territory. Consequently, together with the conflict in a border territory, foreign capital has dried up and the unemployment rate reached 33 percent. During the same year, the country sheltered more than 350,000 refugees from Kosovo (Rossos 2008, 276).

The Kosovo conflict, resulting in NATO intervention and the partial recognition of Kosovo as an independent state, was used as a pretext by Albanian nationalists living in the northern part of the country to annex these lands to Kosovo and/or to form a Great Albania (Rossos 2008, 280; Phillips 2004, 170). The conflict began in February 2001 with attacks on police and military forces; and in summer, there were fears of the civil war (Rossos 2008, 280). After the intervention of the European Union and the United States, the conflict was settled by the Ohrid Agreement. According to it, the Albanian minority received the right to use Albanian language in districts with an ethnic Albanian majority, greater representation in different political and civil institutions, and stronger local self-government.

According to censuses, the Albanian population was and remains second largest in the country. The Yugoslavian census of 1981 shows that the country's citizens were 67 percent Macedonian and 19.8 percent Albanian, followed by Turks at 4.5 percent, Serbs and Roma at 2.3 percent each, Vlachs at 0.3, and others at 3.8 percent (Roudometof 2002, 176). The next statistical reports of 1991, 1994, and 2001 showed similar numbers; the Albanian minority had slight growth by several percentage, and Macedonians ranged from 65 to 67 percent. However, the 2011 census failed because of ethnic disputes; Albanian political representatives claimed that the Macedonian majority commission had arranged criteria to underestimate the number of Albanians in the country. The census did not include the large number of people living abroad for more than one year.[10] The initiative of October 2014 proposed creating a special count in the passport for residents of Macedonia who work abroad but come home at least once a year, but no such official data exist thus far.

In February 26, 2004, during the presidential elections, President Boris Trajkovski died in an airplane crash, and the second round of new presidential elections were won by Branko Crvenkovski as his successor; he remained president until 2009. Since then, the president has been Gjorge Ivanov.

The political climate of the last 10 years has been formed by the IMRO-DPMNE Party, which has the majority of the seats in parliament and has right-wing nationalist positions (Janev 2011, 34). The party is using the radical ethno-nationalist perspective in constructing the national history and establishing the roots of the contemporary Macedonian nation at the time of Alexander the Great as the cradle of the nation (Janev 2011, 35).

Montenegro

When describing the final decade of the existence of socialist Yugoslavia , the collapse in the 1990s and conflicts, the history of Montenegro is closely tied to that of Serbia. Being the smallest republic, with 600,000 inhabitants, with the stagnant economy and weakening communist leadership, the mountainous country was ill-equipped to deal with the growing Belgrade nationalist sentiment. The Serbian nationalist sympathizers, both intellectuals and church leaders, were broadly using the discourse of Serbian ethnic identity to which Montenegrins were automatically included. Montenegrins together with Bosniaks and Macedonians were viewed as Serbians who through the ages have developed their different national identities but historically belong to the titular nation. The notion that Montenegrins were Serbs became *de rigueur* during the 1980s in Serbia and, as Morrison observed (2009, 82), did not find the strong rejection in Montenegro.

---

[10] Macedonia Albanians Propose End to Census Logjam, BalkanInsight, October 6, 2014, http://www.balkaninsight.com/en/article/macedonia-albanians-propose-census-change

A "Milosevic-backed travelling band of nationalist agitators" (Morrison 2009, 83) was spreading through the country and found the grateful listeners, vulnerable due to the worsening economic conditions and seeking easy solutions. The protests for social justice transformed into a demand for ethnic justice and contains such slogans as "Long live the Serbian leadership!," or "Slobodan, you Serb son, when will you come to Cetinje?!," and others. The local communist leaders were losing their power in the country even though they had a support from authorities in Ljubljana, Zagreb, and Sarajevo. The political changes in Eastern Europe and the disintegration of the League of Communists of Yugoslavia in January 1990 forced the country to introduce multiparty elections the same year and, consequently, at the end of the year, 20 parties, 3 political associations, and 1 political movement were registered.

The majority of the seats (83 of 125) was won by the Montenegrin League of Communists, which later changed its name to the Democratic Party of Socialists (DPS). The party was tolerant toward the rising nationalism, even if some of the members were uncomfortable with it.

The elections brought a number of populist parties sympathetic to the "Mother Serbia" rhetoric, including Narodna Stranka Crne Gore (People's Party of Montenegro or NS) with its leader Novak Kilibarda, a professor of Serbian literature using the xenophobic and extreme rhetoric; Narodna Demokratska Stranka (People's Democratic Party), Srpska Radikalna Stranka (Serbian Radical Party) led by Branko Kostic, and the "movement" Pokret za Autonomni Pristup Crne Gore u Srbiju (The Movement for Montenegro's Autonomous Accession in Serbia) (Morrison 2009, 88).

In September 1991, Montenegrin troops that were part of the Yugoslav army entered Croatia and became infamous for the military action at the UNESCO heritage city of Dubrovnik and the Konavle region. The countries' authorities chose a strategy of mass hysteria based on fear, for which media propaganda became a method of influence. Not surprisingly, Montenegrin president Momir Bulatovic called the intervention on the Croatian territory as a legitimate defense of the Socialist Federal Republic of Yugoslavia (Morrison 2009, 91). Anti-Croat propaganda became a part of the everyday life. The statements as "Prevlaka je nasa!" (Prevlaka is ours!)

(town in Croatia) or warnings of Ustashas on the border were massively used at the daily newspaper *Pobjeda* (Morrison 2009, 93) and on TV. Twenty-three years later, in 2014, similar methods would be implemented by Russia toward Ukraine, for which the ghosts of World War II nationalists became the core idea of the anti-Ukrainian propaganda. The intervention will be justified and Crimea will also become "ours." The national media and TV again became a powerful instrument of propaganda for the further justification of war.

Not surprisingly, military intervention was promoted to defend Serbia and Montenegro from the Croatian fascists. Moreover, the restoration of the borders became a legitimate public narrative for the official leaders of the country. Thus, Prime Minister Milo Djukanovic suggested making a new demarcation line with Croatia arguing that "the current border had been designed by 'semi-skilled Bolshevik cartographers' " (Morrison 2009, 92). Furthermore, the Montenegrins saw themselves "not as aggressors, but as defenders of Montenegro and Yugoslavia, who would free the people of the Dubrovnik region from the imposition of fascist rule" (Morrison 2009, 93) and, therefore, many did mobilize voluntarily.

Ironically, the war psychosis usually finishes in much the same way: the protagonists reject the crimes they have committed. Thus, for instance, Svetozar Marović, the influential speaker of the parliament at the period of military intervention who coined the term "War for Peace" has called the damage to Dubrovnik in the documentary film *Rat za mir* (War for Peace) as "a great historical misunderstanding" (Morrison 2009, 97).

On March 1, 1992, the referendum on the status of the country took place. The question was formulated in such way: "Do you agree that Montenegro, as a sovereign republic, should continue to exist in the joint country of Yugoslavia, on a completely equal basis with other republics who wish to do so?" (Morrison 2009, 104); 95.7 percent of the 66 percent of Montenegrins who voted answered positively, and on April 27, 1992, Montenegro and Serbia formed a new state: the Federal Republic of Yugoslavia (FRY). The liberal block of parties formed the Udruzena Opozicija (United Opposition) that presented the interests of Albanians (who were living in

Tuzi area and Ulcinj), Bosniaks (mostly from Sandzak region), and Montenegrins who were against the war and union with Serbia. They were organizing protests and established an independent newspaper but had relatively weak support of a mere 7–9 percent of the population (Morrison 2009, 110).

The xenophobic hysteria provoked the ethnic attacks and vandalism toward the Muslim community. Thus, according to Helsinki Watch, during 1991–92 "around 800 Muslims were banished, kidnapped or murdered" by "extremist inhabitants, members of the Army of Yugoslavia and the police of Montenegro" (Morrison 2009, 121). Many had to find refuge in Turkey, Macedonia, or Western Europe.

After the fall of the Milosevic regime, the presidential elections took place on October 7, 2000, and the opposition leader Vojislav Kostunica was elected. Milosevic refused to accept the results and the anti-Milosevic protests took place at Belgrade. The military did not support the former leader and Kostunica became the president. Next year, in January, the first non-communist prime minister, Zoran Dindic, was elected as the prime minister of Serbia; he would be killed by snipers in March 2003. In March 2002, Serbia and Montenegro signed an agreement for greater autonomy for each other and accepted a new name for the country as "the State Union of Serbia and Montenegro" (Schuman 2004, 63).

Following the peaceful separation in 2001 after the referendum on independence, Montenegro emphasized its interest in EU integration as a political goal (Dzankic 2013, 111). In 2010, it gained the status of candidate country; however, the high levels of corruption, economic problems, and other issues prevent the country from entering the EU.

Conclusions

The dissolution of Yugoslavia was an event of great magnitude that has its origins in a mix of different causes and has tremendously influenced the life of its inhabitants, international relations, and the map of Europe (Flere 2014, 81). "Not only did the breakup have considerable implications for the social, economic and political life in its successor states and the political makeup of the wider region, but it also shaped the international political stage that was emerging from the Cold War" (Vladisavljević 2014, 67). Staring with the predominantly peaceful protests that were occurring throughout the country, bloody civil wars erupted. The assessment of the recent past, the role of the elites, and the nature of the conflicts remain matters of academic discussions. The facts of dissolution, disintegration, or breakup heavily influence the interpretation of the socialist past. The dissolution as a historical event took many scholars by surprise and gave birth to the contradictory explanations and even a different definition of the countries of their origin. One good illustration of such rapid transformation might be the case of major Slovenian social and political studies journal *Teorija in Praksa* (Theory and Practice); in the same year but in different issues, two articles appeared, referring to two different political entities. One was on " 'the perspectives of political pluralism in Yugoslavia', as if Yugoslavia were an unquestionable frame of references" (Flere 2014, 81), the other on " 'the geopolitical and military political position of Slovenia', as if Slovenia were the only natural frame of reference" (Ibid.).

However, if the historical uncertainty or polarity of interpretations in the period of changes is a clear trend, the way scholars are analyzing the period and what issues become central to them depends on the actualized frameworks of the time. Thus, in the 1990s, the well-established scholars were focusing predominantly on the disintegration of Yugoslavia with focus on comprehensive explanations; the second generation of the scholars, emerging in the 2000s, is focusing more on the specific dimensions or contributing factors of the breakup (Vladisavljević 2014, 68–69). Susan Woodward, John Allock, or Sabina Ramet are prominent members of the first generation, and Dejan Jovic or Jasna Dragovic-Soso from the second (Ibid.). Consequently, from the accumulation of the newest research and its further specialization, the possibility of representing the "history of Yugoslavia" as an introductory chapter to the empirical research seems to be a far-fetched, if not impossible, task. Therefore, we consider this chapter to be a brief sketch with accents that might be relevant at the museums of former Yugoslav territories.

As a final summary, one might consider Yugoslavia as a multidimensional space of different time and space-related issues. From its creation to collapse, the federation experienced many changes in its sociocultural, economic, and political spheres. It came through the Stalinist inheritance to the reorientation toward Western markets and cooperation with the non-aligned countries, from prohibition of any religious activity to maintaining the Muslim community, from Yugo-patriotic songs to the "black" parody that balanced on the knife edge between "ridiculous" and "horrible."

With the complex problems in economics and politics and the growth of nationalistic rhetoric, Yugoslavia ended its existence and stepped on the path of hatred and violent dissolution. It went from being a country with the highest per capita income in comparison to the neighboring socialist countries to being the site of political conflict that led to violent warfare (Mehmeti 2013, 189).

With this chapter, we finish with the theoretical aspects of the research questions and are moving to the empirical part. In the previous chapters, the theoretical aspects of representation of the history in the museums has been discussed. I have also presented a brief theoretical background on the history of Yugoslavia as well as provided description of the chosen methodology. The subsequent part of the text is the space of the empirical answers that I wanted to investigate.

5 EMPIRICAL PART

As already mentioned, museums located in the capitals of the countries were chosen for the study. In these cities, museums with main scientific profile is related to the representation of either the socialist period or, more broadly, the contemporary history of the twentieth century was in favor for my observations. If such museums were not available in the countries, I visited the national history museum and verified whether it represents the given period or not and, if so, in what way. The field study was conducted in November and December 2013, and some additional information was collected in January and February 2014.

5.1 Macedonia

Macedonia is experiencing an active phase of construction and fixation of its image through cultural institutions and monuments. Skopje is in the middle of a memory boom. Monuments surround the pedestrian during his or her way through the city center: they lie in wait on the bridges, sometimes they block the way, disguised under the fountains, look out from the roofs of the reconstructed buildings to other monuments located down near the river. A 22-meter high statue of Alexander the Great has become the keeper of contested equilibrium; it is felt that in the case of his displacement from the post, the whole construct of monument codes would collapse. The public space of Skopje has become a field of symbolic struggle (Janev 2011, 9). In combination with the absence of historical chronology in representation, the urban landscape of the city center is missing from the orientation of a consonant architectural style.

> "Over a dozen new buildings designed in an historicist and eclectic mishmash of Neoclassical and Neo-Baroque styles are being erected, facades of the adjacent modern buildings are to be redecorated and adorned with Baroque ornaments .... Over a hundred monuments and sculptures are being installed within the radius of one kilometre, none of them less than four metres high and perched on a pedestal some 12 metres above the ground" (Janev 2011, 8).

The problem is the dissonant architectural styles, materials, and narratives that led the city to being "transformed into Las Vegas and Disneyland" (Graan 2013, 171). The construction of the international image and attraction of the tourists, which was the main goal of the project, is heavily criticized by the opposition due to the problem of national authenticity and damage of the national image (Graan 2013, 171).

The present image of the city was laid in 2010 with the beginning of the realization of the state project called "Skopje 2014." The organizer of the project, the Government of the Republic of Macedonia, has spent the sum of €200–500 million over four years. The government made their first-ever report in April 2012, after local elections, and stated that a sum of 208 million euros has been spent for the reconstructions of the buildings and monuments so far.[11] However, some of the experts think that the sum was much higher and varied around 500 million euros or even more.[12]

The tension between the state and the critical public led to several protests. Thus, in 2009, a group of students of the faculty of architecture, who called themselves "First Arhi (Architect) Brigade" organized a protest via Facebook against the construction of an Orthodox church based on public financing on the main square of Skopje.[13] However, when the students arrived at the square at the appointed time, "[a] crowd of church supporters carrying flags and crosses," was already there.[14] Church supporters came in buses organized for these purposes; police were present but did not intervene in the conflict when the "supporters" came into clash with the students.[15] Later, on a local TV show, protesters were called, "gays and atheists."[16] The given conflict was reflected by the opposition media as a clear intervention of the state to the freedom of opinion and as usage of the state recourse to mobilize the pro-governmental position. The mainstream media presented the protest as having a political background, as

---

11 http://www.balkaninsight.com/en/gallery/skopje-2014

12 Ibid.

13 https://globalvoices.org/2009/03/31/macedonia-student-protest-ends-in-violence/

14 Violence Disrupts Student Protests in Skopje: http://history-of-macedonia.com/2009/03/30/violence-disrupts-student-protests-in-skopje/

15 Ibid.

16 Ibid.

the student protest was led by the daughter of the SDSM presidential candidate the main opposition party to the VMRO-DPMNE.

It was not the single protest activity; for instance, there was a group called "Razpeani Skopjani" (Singing Skopjeans), who repeatedly gathered in central spaces in the city in order to sing children's songs with new lyrics that parodied "Skopje 2014" (Janev 2011). Another symbolic protest was organized by scholars (Mijalkovic and Urbanek) who published a volume in English with the provocative title "Skopje: The World's Bastard," which critically referred to the Skopje 2014 project's "spatial and representational politics" (Graan 2013, 174).

The center is not designed in a single style and has brought much criticism from the side of different expert groups. Some call it historicist kitsch,[17] some a theme park[18] or megalomaniacal project[19] and criticize the whole project as being misplaced, during the economic crisis and high-unemployment rate in the country.

The sculptural line includes the "antiquization" policy as a major direction, continues with the commemoration of the leaders of anti-Islamic rebellions of the Ottoman period, goes further to displaying the National Awakening period (mid-nineteenth to early twentieth century) and diminishes the socialist heritage (Graan 2013, 161). Monuments are either the personalized form of the commemoration of some period or event or a sign that refers to the abstract concept of the long struggle for Macedonian independence. All of the heroes are meant to reflect their Macedonian ethnic origins, which excludes the ethnicity and multiple identities of other ethnic groups together with the Ottoman-era architecture.

The project is materializing the "nostalgia for the presocialist period" (Graan 2013, 169), both in the aspect of choosing the heroes and the style of reconstruction (Lafazanovski 2006, 67). The active or even the dominant role of the government in this trajectory is rarely discussed. "The government tries to erase the communist past from the visual appearance

---

17 http://edition.cnn.com/2011/10/04/world/europe/macedonia-skopje-2014/index.html

18 Ibid.

19 http://www.balkaninsight.com/en/article/macedonian-culture-strategy-milestone-or-wish-list

and replace it with the pre-socialist facade that would be reminiscent of a full European integration" (Mattioli 2014, 83).

Being part of broader entities, Macedonia did not have its independence until recently and as a nearly established country, it faces the problem of the rising right to include the famous persons of world history or history, which is already formed in neighboring countries in their national narrative. In other words, there is a debate on the nationalization of the hero and making it "Macedonian." Such example consists of the monument of Justinian I, Tsar Samuil (Samuel of Bulgaria), and Philip II of Macedon Alexan (Photo 5.19). The inconsistency of the situation may be represented by the "main" statue in the central square. Officially, it is called the "Warrior on a Horse," which was unveiled in September 2011 to symbolize 20 years of the country's independence. That title is rarely used, but the statue is commonly known and called as the statue of the Alexander the Great.[20] During his visit to the London School of Economics, Macedonian foreign minister Nikola Poposki stated that Macedonia wants "to be real, economic partners."[21] However, as critically remarks author of the interview Tena Prelec[22]: "the towering 33-m high statue depicting Alexander the Great—which the government claims to be 'just any' warrior on a horse—seems to contradict this statement."

[20] http://www.theguardian.com/world/2011/aug/14/alexander-great-macedonia-warrior-horse

[21] http://blogs.lse.ac.uk/lsee/2014/06/13/poposki-we-dont-want-to-win-against-greece-we-want-to-be-real-partners/

[22] http://theprotocity.com/brand-old-skopje/

Photo 5.1: Main Square, Skopje, December 2013

Other examples are the statues of Saints Cyril and Methodius, who were born in ninth-century Thessalonica, Byzantine Empire and Mother Teresa, born in Skopje, Ottoman Empire and being of Albanian origin.

In the example of the spatial image of Skopje, Janev (2011, 3) shows how the "ethnocratic regime," which is understood as "ruptur[ing] the concept of the demos in favor of a single ethno-national group" has emerged in Macedonia recently. The loss of democratization in the 1990s is replaced with the "ethnic bargaining between ethnic elites. De facto, Macedonia is a binational country, where the rule of law and "separation of power" are not working (Vankovska 2013, 99).

As shown by Trpevska and Micevski (2014, 308), there is a visible intervention of the state in the media sphere and economics. The deterioration of the democratic initiatives, the intervention of the state on different levels and the politicizing of the past led to the "continuous movement towards authoritarianism" (Trpevska and Micevski 2014, 308; Prelec 2014). "Macedonian political life has been reduced to the activities of ethnopolitical parties .... The Albanians who form the second largest ethnic group in the country are not inactive, passive onlookers in this spatial reordering" (Janev 2011, 8). They also follow this trend. Thus, in January 2012, the leader of the most influential Albanian party, the Democratic Union for Integration (the second largest party after VMRO-DPMNE), inaugurated the construction of Skanderbeg Square and the monument of Skanderbeg, the greatest Albanian national hero (Janev 2011, 9). The given party has emerged as a transformation of the National Liberation Army that ignited the military confrontation in 2001. "The total dominance of ethnopolitical parties and their respective policies and public discourse lead to the conclusion that Macedonia has stepped out of democracy into ethnocracy" (Janev 2011, 9), and Skopje 2014 is the representation of this politics through the urban social landscape.

Paradoxically, Macedonian nationalism was constructed, encouraged, and implemented with the dominant help of Yugoslav governance. "The Socialist Republic of Macedonia, as part of the Yugoslav Federation, was formally encouraged to develop a national identity that would distinguish it from the neighbouring republics" (Dimova 2012, 238). In 1945, official Macedonian orthography was implemented, the language was distinguished from Bulgarian by the efforts of the Yugoslav linguists who selected the central Vardar dialect as a central point.

Together with the construction of language, a unique national identity was implemented by the constructionist power of scientists. Consequently, the Yugoslav project encouraged the emergence of a Macedonian national identity; however, it was oppressing "the nationalist claims to the larger region of Macedonia Antiquizacija and the Greek-Macedonian Conflict" (Dimova 2012, 238) as not relevant to the geopolitical needs.

After the disintegration of Yugoslavia, FYROM continued the rhetoric of Macedonian uniqueness and non-similarity to its neighboring countries; but at the same time, the socialist period that had constructed the discursive preconditions for such statements was disappearing. Simultaneously, previously forbidden statements of Macedonian antiquization were expanded through the political narratives and became actual in 1999 when VMRO-DPMNE came into power. When the same party was reelected in 2007, their "clear agenda to enforce and purify the national identity of the country, by undertaking a number of activities in the domain of culture" became visible (Dimova 2012, 238).

The contemporary Macedonian "monument boom" phenomena, which requires a broad separate study in order to show that the exclusion of Yugoslavia from the "heritage map" of the "worth mentioning" periods of the past is clearly confirmed by the overall state politics involved in the discourse of antiquization (Langer and Lechler 2010, 42) of the country and tied to the discourse of nationalization of the transnational memory. In the following section, I aim to demonstrate how such politics intervenes into the museum space and how it deals with the socialist past.

The analysis is based on the study of two main history institutions: the recently established Museum of the Macedonian Struggle, and the oldest institution in the country, the History Museum. It will be shown how differently the Yugoslav period can be represented in the same city, and how clearly it is interdependent with the political sphere.

The Museum of the Macedonian Struggle

The capital city has six main museums. The core one is the Museum of the Macedonian Struggle, located at the center of the city. It has a perfect location: the heart of the city, near the main bridge. From one side, there is a tourist attraction, the Old Town; from the other, the main square; on the left is the National Theatre and the Holocaust Memorial Centre for the Jews of Macedonia. Thirty metres away is the Archaeological Museum, which opened its doors in October 2014, after reconstruction (Photo 5.1).

Photo 5.2: Archeological Museum, Skopje, December 2013

The Holocaust Museum is also a newly established institution and is in a good condition both internally and externally. Near these museums is the National Gallery, which was reorganized from the Hamam building, the public Turkish sauna. It is important to describe the location of the institution that is being observed because in the following text, it will become clear that the conditions of other historical museums in the same city dramatically differ: they are subject to obscurity, whether they are still open or already closed for an indefinite period.

The whole title of the museum is rather long but very symptomatic: "Museum of the Macedonian Struggle for Sovereignty and Independence—Museum of VMRO—Museum of the Victims of the Communist Regime" (Photo 5.2). It opened its doors in September 2011 as part of the "Skopje 2014" project.

Photo 5.3: Museum of Macedonian Struggle, Skopje, December 2013

The staff of the Museum of Macedonian Struggle has a clear division of responsibilities according to which everybody is allocated tasks: security, ticket office, tour guides. This may seem like an obvious fact, but it is not in comparison to the situation in some other museums in Skopje. Thus, in the Macedonian History Museum, one will find the security guard who also serves as a ticket seller and an information officer.

The museum's subject is the representation of the battles and uprisings organized by Macedonian people, which are interpreted as the long-term process of the Macedonian fight for independence. The victimization throughout history and the glorification of the imagined national community are the main tools provided by the museum. It is not surprising that the Yugoslav period is reduced to the only issue of imprisonment at Goli Otok (Naked Island), sadly known for being used as a place of political imprisonment (Photos 5.4. and 5.5). The exhibition specified the period of 1945–56 as the time framing of the display and is the only mention of Yugoslavia at this museum. The nodal point that construct the discourse is the document that illustrates the condemnation. The waxwork of the bureaucrat sitting at the table, stamps, and other stationery items serve to create the context of injustice and ideologically motivated distribution of power. Such elements articulated by the oral narration provided by the guide are transformed into moments—the polysemic elements with fixed meaning.

Photo 5.4: Brochure sold at the shop of the Museum of Macedonian Struggle, Skopje, December 2013

Photo 5.5: Section from the brochure titled "Victims of the Communist Regime," Skopje, December 2013

The reduction of a broad layer of the recent history into a single issue works as the best explicit illustration of the non-neutrality of the museum, as well as of its ideological constructionist power.

The main visual instruments to be used for demonstrations are panoramic pictures and wax statues, both of which are newly made. Panoramic pictures concentrate on displaying battles; statues accentuate the individuals taking part in the battle. All of the panoramic pictures were made by Ukrainian and Russian painters. Afterward, during my talk with a guide, I asked why there were no Macedonian painters and was told that in contrast to those nations' long-term panoramic tradition, the Macedonian one is not developed. Perhaps, that was a reference to the socialist Soviet art inheritance.

All materials are constructing believe in the existence of the national community with its organic aspiration to be independent. It is important to mention that the only way to visit the museum is to have a guided tour. Tours can be provided in both Macedonian and English. Perhaps, at the beginning, this idea was meaningful but was spoiled when implemented because the visitors are not able to spend even a minute after the guided tour has finished walking through the exhibition on their own: to read the plaques, to see considered artefacts and stands. When the tour is over all are obliged to leave the exposition hall together with the guide. An additional inconvenience is the ongoing flow of people following their guide. If two groups appeared in one room, one of the guides tries to present the material more quickly in order to go to the next hall. Such a situation not only leads to the reduction of the material but creates the impression both of a conveyor belt and a Disneyland attraction.

In the described situation, the visitor becomes the object of ideological manipulations because he or she is limited in his or her rights and time spending. The visitor does not have time to read the plaques, to observe carefully the material, to have as much time as he or she personally wants to spend at the museum. This produces the feeling of being on a conveyor belt; the diversity of images and fullness of pseudo-artefacts that surround the visitor, who has however limited time to see it and has to move on, make the exhibition look like a Disneyland attraction. In Disneyland, the visual imagery that surrounds the visitor is made for helping him or her to feel in some imaginary time and place. The objects and the whole picture do not intend to represent the real world; the items do not need to be original. The whole entourage is done as an extra bonus for the main goal: delivering adrenaline and feeling certain emotions. Museums initially had another main goal: to display unique, exotic, and important artefacts. At the Macedonian museum, originality and authenticity are replaced with the creation of the atmosphere with the model "pretend to believe it was so." Due to this aspect, the museum has similarities to Disneyland.

The logical completion of the conveyor type of exhibition is the reduced role of the guide, who, although an insider, does not know or does not see as possible to share information on the plans of the museum. I did not succeed in determining the guide's personal opinion on the presented topic, on the politics of the museum, and even on the plans for the upcoming exhibitions. I received answers that showed the limited responsibilities that the guides had. They were not aware of any information regarding the new exhibition, which at the moment of my observation was literally under the noisy reconstruction of the last floor where none of the visitors were allowed to go. All answers were reduced to the formula: "I have no idea what will be there; I'm the guide and can answer the questions about history."

In this way, the limitation of functions, the vertical model of decision making without taking into consideration the guide's opinions on the displayed period (who then work as social agents of spreading the verified and standardized information), and the conveyer type of presentation makes the museum seem to be the visible instrument of the state's ideology. In this regard, the reduction of the Yugoslav period (the recent past of the country) into the narrative of repressions works as the instrument for creating the image of independence as a teleological development. Such an approach of displaying history sends dangerous signals because the orientation of the museum includes the showing of history in an ideologically correct manner into its main function as opposed to merely showing history. Being a national museum subsidized from the national budget, we may conclude that the museum does not have its independent policy in producing knowledge and is closely bound by requests from the ruling VMRO-DPMNE political party in "leveraging nationalistic sentiments and partially recreating the history of their own party, while reaffirming themselves as the true bearers of the Macedonian spirit" (Prelec 2014). The erasure of the socialist past, which is visible in the architectural scope of the city (Graan 2013; Mattioli 2014) is paralleled in the museum with the reduced model of referring to Yugoslavia as a "prison of the nations" and Tito as a tyrant.

Museum of Macedonia

It was rather difficult to find this museum. It is located at the periphery of the Old Centre in the area where elderly men drink Turkish tea in the street cafés. Even when I found the street where the museum was located, it was still problematic to recognize the building as a cultural institution dealing with heritage because of the somewhat neglected appearance and the unusual social practices carried out in front of it. Children were playing football on the spontaneously organized football field just in front of the museum (Photo 5.6). The presence of children having their outdoor activities works as an indicator of the forsakenness of this public space. Due to the special status of the museums as a DNA of the national heritage, the common unspoken rules are regenerating their aura such as not to have unauthorized activities around the place. Additionally, football is related to such sort of activities that need much space that won't be disturbed by pedestrians and possess a risk for damaging the neighboring buildings. All of this allows us to conclude that there are not many visitors to the museum and that it has a marginalized position compared to other similar institutions.

The museum is the oldest in the country. It was opened in 1924 and consists of three parts: archaeological, historical, and ethnological museums.

The practice of smoking inside the buildings, even at the museum buildings where special temperature conditions have to be provided, is widespread among the security guards at several museums we have visited. I would interpret it as an additional sign that the institution has ceased to work according to its functions, lost its social significance, and consequently requires reorganization.

Photo 5.6: Entrance to the Museum of Macedonia, Skopje, December 2013

The historical part is located at the two-story building, quite huge, but urgently in need of renovations. It lacks light and order. The only prominent exposition was dedicated to the orthodox icons (Photo 5.7); it was organized with the financial support of the European Union. This information was specified on the huge plaques near the entrance and constantly repeated on the plaques accompanying the exposition. The area had a special temperature regime and inscriptions in Macedonian and English. The icons might be auspicious material to represent because it is easy to change the perception of the religious objects into the other nonreligious connotation, by putting them into the discourse of cultural or world heritage. Such a tendency also allows avoiding reinterpretations of the history. A specific example will follow when the Yugoslav period will be described. However, the non-visibility of the similar heritage of the Islamic culture might be a clear element of the politics of exclusion and cultural dominance of a single national narrative. Especially, it might be questioned at the museum, which is physically located in the area of the Ottoman architectural visual regime, whose silence is rapidly intervened from time to time by the call to prayer from the mosque adjacent to the building.

Photo 5.7: Collection of Orthodox Icons, Museum of Macedonia, Skopje, December 2013

Contemporary science frequently discusses the idea of the museum as a space of inclusion of the broader audience; this is not the case of the given institution, at least at the moment of observation. The museum works in the opposite way: the exclusion of minority interests, the absence of the history that might be interesting to them, and the concentration on the singularity.

The next room demonstrates the liberation movement of 1878 and the Ottoman Empire period. Some plaques are only in Macedonian; some are duplicated in English. As becomes clear from the plaques, the Ottoman period has a negative connotation while the central focus of the exposition is the liberation from it.

Finally, we move into the rooms of the greatest interest for us: the representation of the socialist period. The idea of the exhibition can be described in two words: "gloriously positive." Yugoslavia is shown as a peaceful time, a time full of optimism for the future. The exposition starts with the stands showing the period of the fight against Nazism during World War II with the glorification of the Macedonian Partisan movement together with mentions of the partisans of the whole of Yugoslavia. Attributing the selective number of characteristic to the homogenized group of "partisans" (brave, courageous, masculine), the controversial characteristics remains for all other groups. In such a way, the mechanism of typifications maintains the secured construction of reality and allows to have stable hegemonic discourse.

After several stands presenting the World War II period, the public space continues to narrate in a rather chaotic way chronologically unbounded topics. There emerge stands about the nineteenth-century Macedonian national movement and then followed by artefacts from 1925: the first officially published book in Greece on the Macedonian language. After that come again stands telling about World War II, Holocaust and it is followed by illustrations of "the spirit of progress" during the first socialist postwar period. Parts of the physical space lack any expositions at all: they were taken away once and now have been left with empty walls. World War II and Yugoslav sectionstands are clearly glorifying those periods. It is happening because the exposition has not been subjected to any changes since the socialist period: old plaques, an old style ("socialist type") narrative (glorification and typical phrases: "comrades" etc.), old (slightly faded) pictures make me think that the place is no longer used. It lacks very basic financial support and is experiencing times of uncertain transition. A coincidence, which cannot be understood as representative knowledge, however, confirms our statement. I would like to mention an artefact that has appeared in my hands the same day. I bought a plate with the title "Macedonia" on it. The seller wrapped it with a piece of newspaper. On a closer inspection, the article in a newspaper was informing the reader about the disappearance of 47 golden artefacts from the museum I had recently visited. The article described the lamentable state of the museum, which lacks financial support and renovation (The Morning newspaper (Утрински весник), November 8, 2013, 3).

All given observations help to understand the museum as being stuck in an unclear division. It needs reorganization of the expositions, refreshment of the stands, the addition of the factual material, and the systematizing of space (Photos 5.8 and 5.9). The building and the exposition inside seems to be currently frozen; consequently, the Yugoslav version of the historical representation without the switch to the revisionist national narrative of the independent Macedonia remains.

At the moment of observation, I was the only visitor to the museum. According to the guide whom I have found in the section of ethnography, there could be approximately 80–100 visitors per day. To my question or rather a sad sympathy regarding the feeling of neglect and visibility of no financial support, my interlocutor answered, "I don't know what to answer ... They are there, and we are here." The feeling that the museum has been neglected remained with me during the whole visit. The guide said that at the current moment another institution, the Archaeological Museum, which is now under reconstruction, takes all funding.

Photo 5.8: Inside view, Museum of Macedonia, Skopje, December 2013

Photo 5.9: Inside view, Museum of Macedonia, Skopje, December 2013

Conclusions

Yugoslavia is presented through the non-revised exposure of World War II. It finishes with the occurrence of the Second Yugoslavia and, hence, the Yugoslav period as a period that ceased to exist is absent.

Analyzing these two museums, we may draw the following conclusions. The complex presentation of the Yugoslav period is not favorable for the recent construction of the contemporary history project. By itself, by the matter of historical fact of Macedonian history, Yugoslavia is not an actual period to concentrate on. Yugoslavia is needed as auxiliary material for establishing some broader picture or concept of history, being largely ordered by the state. The Museum of the Macedonian Struggle selects the piece from very broad and complex period and reduces it to the single issue: political imprisonment. Hence, Yugoslavia is represented with the minus sign, as a kind of horrible short sleep, which the individual wants to escape from having to recollect it. Another museum, the Museum of Macedonia, which demonstrates the researched period in a glorious way, goes into oblivion with the lack of funding and its interpretation of Yugoslavia follows it. Yugoslavia's removal of favor fit into the broader issue of the cityscape image and related to the national identity construction through the visual texture of the city.

Both museums avoid inclusions of national minorities. On the one hand, it fits the politics of homogenizing the Macedonian identity; on another, it does not stress any actual history for Albanian minority that constitutes more than 30 percent of the whole population.

The imagination of Yugoslavia as a country with a stable economy and as the relatively secure period was the matter of the pre-independence politics of representation but is not actual anymore. The period after World War II is inscribed into the canvas of the narration, but the circumstances of such presentation are simply the lack of financial support to reorganize the exposition. The History Museum that ties with such vision is experiencing the lack of financial support and, hence, cannot be analyzed as an important player that indicates the state policy.

The hypothesis that was provided at the beginning of the research was not confirmed. The representation of the Yugoslav period became opposite to what we expected to see. The association with a stable economy and high level of security was not seen. The second hypothesis about the representation of the post–World War II period as the time of reconstruction of the city and the demonstration of the collective spirit was partially confirmed, while being represented only in one of the two museums. The explanation of the findings that were observed and that contradict the hypotheses lies in the political sphere. The Macedonian case demonstrated how the active involvement of the political actors allows constructing the historical narrative based on the selectivity and on the emphasis on the authoritarian nature of the former regime for the construction of their own image as a legitimate alternative.

5.2 Kosovo

There are two main museums: Kosovo Museum and Ethnographic Museum. All museums in Pristina have the politics of no entrance fee. Being entities subordinated by the public institution, they are state-funded. Both museums are located in close distance to each other, are in good condition, and look as been recently renovated. The central area in which both museums are located consist of the buildings constructed during Ottoman occupation. During SFRY, it worked as a nature museum; in the middle of 1990s, it was closed and finally reorganized and seriously renovated in 2003. In the vicinity of museums, King's Mosque is the most visible neighboring building. Also, there is a nineteenth-century clock tower and residential town houses. The Ethnographic Museum belonged to the wealthy Albanian family and was constructed at the beginning of the nineteenth century (Basha 2007). Now, the museum is called in both ways: as an ethnographic museum and as Emin Gjiku complex using initials of the historical owner.

Today, the museum works as a place of representation of Albanian traditional cultural heritage. A two-storied building uses the ethnographic approach and concentrates on displaying clothes, crafts, and musical instruments predominantly of the nineteenth century (Photo 5.10). Trying to find the nodal points or the fundamental elements on which the current identity is based, we might say that this construct is based on two main elements. First is the legitimation of traditional Albanian culture as historical background and second is its fixation with the Kosovo war. If Ethnographic Museum is responsible for the first element, Kosovo Museum is dealing with the second. The exclusivist ethnic identification is constructed through the ethnographic museum space as a counter-narrative and its contemporary meaning is displayed through the space of the second museum.

Photo 5.10: Inside view, Ethnographic Museum, Pristina, December 2013

During my observation in Emin Gjiku complex, the space of the museum was used for the lecture. It was Monday, a nonworking day for the visitors, and therefore, the space was easier to transform into an education space. The lecture was given by an invited American lecturer on the museum management issue. The main question which was discussed: how to organize the profitability from the cultural events that take place in the city. The additional luck for me as a researcher was accompanied by the fact that the meeting brought together a relevant audience: museum guides, managers dealing with the cultural events and the heritage of the region. The lecture was followed by the discussions about the situation in the Pristina cultural sphere and has been served to us as sufficient introduction into the pulse of the city and problems which it met.

Extremely important for understanding the problems of the country was the discussion, which arose during the meeting with the key question; and for me, the embodiment of the problem was the following question: where to find public to organize the expositions and cultural events in the city? It was stated that the local public is quite passive and even events of high quality (for instance, the Jazz festival in Kosovo, which brought international musicians together in Pristina) lack a sufficient number of visitors.

Such problem may also be questioned in regard to the museum space and therefore was mentioned above. The second place where our observation was conducted was the Kosovo Museum.

Kosovo museum is the general museum in the city and may be called the main one in the country. It is housed in a nineteenth-century construction and served as the seat of the Ottoman provincial government until 1912. From 1949, it was used as a public museum with the departments of archaeology, ethnography, and natural science. Ten years later, the topic of the National Liberation Struggle was added (Riedlmayer 2000). Originally, the museum was named as the Kosovo Museum (Muzeu I Kosovës/Muzej Kosova i Metohije); in 1990s, the name was reduced to the Pristina Museum (Muzej u Pristini). In 1999, the building was used by the Yugoslav military as an operational headquarters (Ibid.). Many important artefacts were removed to Belgrade museum and are still kept there in the repository. Official Kosovo demand to return the local heritage and this is visible through the postcards produced by the museum, which one can take free of charge. The front page of each postcard represents a single artefact that is still in Belgrade; on the reserve side is written the following words: "We have to return where we belong. Your help needed!" In smaller letters, the following is written: "More than a thousand of pieces of Archeological and ethnological collection of the Museum of Kosovo recollected in 1999 by the Serbian authorities to Belgrade" (Photo 5.11). The symbol of the museum is "Queen of Dardania"; this artefact, which was found in 1955, is dated from the Neolithic era.[23] It is also located in Belgrade.

[23] European Stability Initiative http://www.esiweb.org/index.php?lang=en&id=178

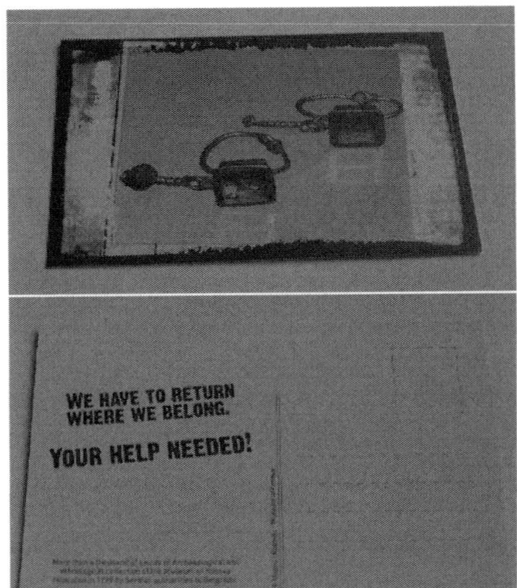

Photo 5.11: Postcard, Museum of Kosovo, Pristina, December 2013

During our conversation with the staff, we were discussing relation with Serbian museums and my interlocutor mentioned that the network relation with the staff of Belgrade museums are developed due to the common international project where both sides are involved. The reason why the artefacts are still there is political. It is addressed to the Belgrade authorities, not to the staff or the director of the museum because such decisions are not under their jurisdiction. The Serbian museum politics is, hence, understood as an object of political games of the state level but not as the initiator of any kind of straight-out expropriation of the museum authorities. Such explanations given by the curators allow us to say that the framework of the recent conflict has transformed into perceiving it as a political game and that the understanding between the two countries on the level of cultural institutions has increased. The role of the international institutions, such as EU and UN, is not to be understated.

At the moment of our observation, there were two exhibitions: temporal and permanent. Permanent exhibition was dedicated to the war of 1999 and NATO support (Photos 5.12 and 5.13). One booth shows the history of a given organization; all plaques are new. The visual regime reminds us of the EU parliament museum and used the standardized plaques.

Photo 5.12: Permanent exhibition, Museum of Kosovo, Pristina, December 2013

Photo 5.13: Permanent exhibition, Museum of Kosovo, Pristina, December 2013

Another exhibition, located on the ground floor at the moment of observation (November 2013), was temporarily rented by an international NGO based in Pristina, which offers their services for the reconstruction of the city (Photo 5.14). The exhibition therefore showed their plans through the modeled posters and served as self-promotion of the NGO.

Photo 5.14 Temporal exhibition, Museum of Kosovo, Pristina, December 2013

I would summarize that the most actual topic of the representation is the recent war in Kosovo from one side and actualized Albanian identity from another. It could be seen through the exhibitions of two museums, where the typical Albanian organization of living is represented in one and the new exhibition dedicated to the Kosovo war in another. Kosovo war is presented in conjunction with the role of NATO and U.S. support. As the main material for representation, high-resolution posters were used. The text is made in Albanian language.

The war, which killed an estimated number of 10,000 people during 1998 and 1999 (Kienzler 2010), clearly became the central aspect of the urban cultural landscape. The majority of the victims were Kosovar Albanians killed by Serbian forces. Additionally, more than 860,000 civilians had to take refuge outside Kosovo and 590,000 were internally displaced (Kienzler 2010).

The role of war memories is difficult to exaggerate. Analyzing the urban landscape, one will notice the predominance of the elements referring to the given period. Monuments, which were reconstructed recently are dedicated to three types of personalities: first, leaders of the resistance movement and of the KLA; second, to American influence; and third, the heroes from the "classic" Albanian history. Thus, mentioning representative of the first group, we have to tell about Ibrahim Rugova's personality. Being leader of the peaceful resistance movement and later the president, he is commemorated through the public monument (Photo 5.15) and a big poster hanging on the main street (Photo 5.16). The KLA leaders are commemorated through Zahir Pajaziti and Adem Jashari personalities. There is a monument dedicated to Pajaziti (Photo 5.17) and poster with Adem Jashari photo on it.

Photo 5.15: Ibrahim Rugova monument, Pristina, December 2013

Photo 5.16: Ibrahim Rugova poster, Pristina, December 2013

Jashari is usually referred as the "father of the KLA," who was participating in attacks against Serbian police, the establishment, and later army. In 1997, he was convicted in terrorism in absentia by a Yugoslav court held in Serbia and afterward Serbian forces attacked his house in Prekaz in March 1998. As the result of the battle that followed, Jashari, his wife, son, and more than 50 other members of his family were killed. Jashari was posthumously awarded the title "Hero of Kosovo" (Perritt 2010: 3), the national theater and airport in Pristina and the stadium in Kosovska Mitrovica were named after him (Elsie 2012, 222).

Now, Jashari's house, located in Prekaz, is one of the most visited memorials in Kosovo with 50 or 60 busloads of visitors arriving during the weekends.[24] Also, it is the only one protected by a special law (Elsie 2012, 222). The place serves both as a museum where Jashari was living before he and his relatives were killed in 1998 by the Serbian army and as a commemoration place of his burial.

[24] Milena Milosevic, Boris Pavelic, Edona Peci, Marija Ristic Ethnic Divisions Set in Stone, June 25, 2013 http://www.balkaninsight.com/en/article/ethnic-divisions-set-in-stone

The second type is represented with a Bill Clinton monument and a monument called "Newborn" (Photo 5.18). The last type is visible through the Scanderbeg monument at the city center (Photo 5.19).

Photo 5.17: Zahir Pajaziti monument, Pristina, December 2013

Photo 5.18: "Newborn" monument, Pristina, December 2013

Photo 5.19: Scanderbeg monument, Pristina, December 2013

The Yugoslavian monument heritage is visible through the object "Monument of Brotherhood and Unity" erected in socialist times. Even though it's located at the city center, it doesn't look good: some of its parts are painted with graffiti and have small damages on the sides. Being a constructionism monolithic type of sculpture, it is easy to get used to not noticing it anymore and to allocate it as a part of the common landscape, to see it as a mechanical obstruction. However, comparing it to other monuments located in the city, we may say that graffiti and some average vandalism are visible on different monuments and therefore cannot be articulated as targeted violation of the narrative that the monuments consist.

Even though, I have pointed out on some trends in monument politics, the role of culture as the key agent of identity construction does not have to be exaggerated. According to Balkan Insight information, from the overall budget of 1.4 billion euro, less than 1 percent was spent on culture in 2010.[25] An additional problem is the high corruption. Thus, Transparency International Corruption Perception Index identified Kosovo and

[25] Shengjyl Osmani, Culture feels Crunch in Cash-Strapped Kosovo, February 24, 2011, http://www.balkaninsight.com/en/article/culture-feels-crunch-in-cash-strapped-kosovo

Albania as the most corrupt countries in Southeast Europe, ranked 110 out of 174 countries.[26]

Pristina does not deal with the Yugoslavian past at the movement; it is not presented and seems Kosovo didn't have it, but such heeling is clear to understand. The posttraumatic city that received its independence has to construct first its national identity, selectively using those imagined times when the routes of the country's nation could be found. These are some "old times" when Albanians were living their traditional life, which is represented at the Ethnographical Museum and the times of war—the point of bifurcation which brought to the emergence of the independent state and which is shown at the Kosovo museum.

Another subject that we think requires attention is the growing intercultural dialogue with the other sides of the recent conflict. The interviews with curators of both museums have shown that workshops and international museum projects, initiated by European Union support, increased museum cooperation between Kosovo and Serbia.

Due to the complex number of reasons, Yugoslavia as an object of representation is not presented in the Pristina museums at the moment. This is not the exclusivist politics of the museum, but rather the state strategy to deal with the "clarified" constructed image, which guarantees financial support of the international organization. As Kostadinova (2011, 13) argued, "the international presence in Kosovo has created a dependency syndrome and the local authorities and society still don't share international community's enthusiasm and commitment to the promotion of culture and cultural heritage." Her statement was dedicated to the situation with the preservation of religious objects in Kosovo, but it seems the dependency syndrome may be applied to the broader context of Kosovo political specificity.

I was not able to either confirm or refute our hypothesis that the socialist period was not represented in Pristina. However, the assumption that the given period would be represented through the authoritarianism, Albanian protests, weak economic condition, and growing Serbian nationalism

---

[26] Transparency International, 2014 results http://www.transparency.org/cpi2014/results

could be used in the future, when the socialist period would be represented. It seems to me that such representation is possible due to the current political strategy based on the centrality of the victimization narration.

Conclusions

The posttraumatic city constructs its national identity, by the usage of imagined past times without referring to the precise historical frames and represent traditional Albanian life through the family relations in the Ethnographical Museum. The nodal points on which the national identity is based are grounded on two main elements. First, as we mentioned is the legitimation of Albanian culture, and second is fixation of this identity in conjunction to the Kosovo war. The Ethnographic Museum is dealing with the first element, Kosovo Museum is responsible for displaying the second. It seems that the exclusivist ethnic identification, which is constructed through the Ethnographic Museum works as a counter-narrative to the narrative of "Serbianism" and anti-Albanianism of the late 1980s and 1990s, and its fixed contemporary meaning is displayed through the space of the Kosovo museum. At the same time, the role of the intermediary institutions has to be mentioned in one more aspect. It allows the growth of the intercultural dialogue with the other sides of the recent conflict. In the summarizing table, I have called the representation of Yugoslavian period a lacuna time, meaning its absence at the both public spaces of the city and museum space in particular.

5.3 Montenegro

After splitting with Serbia due to the results of the 2006 referendum, Montenegro proclaimed its independence on June 3 of the same year. The constitution of 2006 declared Montenegrin the official language of the country, and since then public debates have appeared on the question of the relevance of such formulation. The government is implementing the strengthening politics of the national identity constriction and this is visible in the language politics field. As an example, the introduction of two new phonemes/letters may be mentioned.

Voting for independence, the majority of the population, however, had trouble with identifying themselves as Montenegrins. If in Croatia, there was a visibly clear attitude to identify ethnicity and language as the same (96.12 percent declared their language and ethnicity as Croatian), Montenegrin identity, as well as language identification was and remains today more problematic. According to the 2011 census, 36.97 percent of the population declared that they spoke Montenegrin and 42.88 percent Serbian. At the same time, the majority of the population declared themselves as Montenegrins (44.9 percent) (Felberg and Šarić 2013, 13). Even though, the majority still identifies themselves with Serbian language, the number of those who identify themselves with Montenegrin identity has grown since poll in 2001, as well as the number of Montenegrin speakers has also increased (Felberg and Šarić 2013, 29).

Nevertheless, the problem of self-identification is still very real (Jenne and Bieber 2014). When compared with the year 1948, today's indicator is insignificant; in 1948, 90.68 percent identified themselves as Montenegrins compared to 44.98 percent in 2011 (Jenne and Bieber 2014, 432). The authors have shown that "the decline in the number of Montenegrins was primarily due to a shift in the self-declared identity within the same population" but not due to emigration, fertility rate, or other factors (Ibid., 435). Decrease in Montenegrin self-identification is surprising because the country had a historical memory of independence upon which a national identity could be easily constructed.

What is also interesting to note is the geographical component of differences in self-identification. Between the period of 1991 and 2003, the majority of the inhabitants of northern districts that is bordering on Serbia identified themselves as Serb, while the other parts (central and coastal districts) continued to identify themselves as a Montenegrin (Jenne and Bieber 2014, 436). The role of the national elites is important in understanding the given problem. During the Yugoslavian period, the political elites were effectively mediated between two dichotomies: from one side, stressing the distinctiveness of the Montenegrin identity, from the other, showing its closeness to the Serbian identity (Ibid., 442).

Regions with a high proportion of mixed marriages were predominantly identifying themselves as Yugoslavian, both in the 1981 census, and still 20 percent of them had the same identification by 1991 census. The next census of 2003 and 2011 has shown that 10 percent of inhabitants from same regions were using such option as "other" or "undeclared" (Jenne and Bieber 2014, 447). The problems of identification, according to Jenne and Bieber (2014), can be explained by the logic of situational nationalism. They argue that national identities shift in response to compelling geopolitical battles and "vary significantly over time as a result of changes in state-periphery relations and attendant shifts in the salient political cleavages at the local, national and international levels" (Ibid., 439). Simply speaking, inhabitants of Montenegro received more benefits, identifying themselves with another than federal unit level.

Such approach was visible not only during communism but also during 1990s. Serbian identity was prevailing. Milosevic had toppled the regional leaderships in Montenegro and also Vojvodina and Kosovo by replacing them with loyal pro-Serbian politicians. To such cadres belonged Momir Bulatovic, the president of Montenegro between 1990 and 1998, prime minister Milo Djukanovic between 1991 and 1998, and Svetozar Marović, president of parliament from 1994 until 2001 (Jenne and Bieber 2014, 448). Only during late 1990, when Milosevic and Belgrade politics began to be perceived as a threat, there was growing number of those, who opposed themselves to this politics and therefore identified as Montenegrin. For this reason, as a political trend, in 1997, a section of the Socialist People's Party (SNP) under Djukanovic turned against Milosevic and toward the idea of Montenegro's independence. Today, this party, the former pro-Milosevic element before, presents itself as the advocate of European integration.[27] The ruling party, the Democratic Party of Socialists, is the direct successor of the Yugoslav Communist Party and is still in power. The essential characteristic of transformation period in Montenegro is the continuity of the dominance of the same elites since 1990. In 2003, Bieber noticed that the Democratic Party "is the only party in former Yugoslavia,

[27] http://www.balkaninsight.com/en/article/montenegro-key-political-parties

and across all of the Balkans for that matter, which has managed to maintain power throughout the transition period." Ten years later, in 2014, Kovačević argue the same thing, that the same party is still dominant and that it has significant control over different spheres of life: social, cultural, and artistic. In such a situation, when there were no significant changes in political sphere, even though the former communists have become EU sympathizers, it is interesting to see how the museum sphere reflects the past as a social agent of the state politics.

Podgorica City Museum

The biggest city and the capital of Montenegro is Podgorica, the former Titograd, but the "cultural capital" and heritage center is predominantly contained in the previous capital of the country—Cetinje. In order to see the most holistic picture, we've visited both capitals. Podgorica hosts several museums dealing with historical issues: the Podgorica City Museum, the Marko Miljanov Museum, and the Natural History Museum. The last one deals with flora and fauna, and the second represents some aspects of life of the nineteenth-century Podgorica. The Podgorica City Museum tries to combine the history of the city through the ages, by creating the cut-off point in the Middle Paleolithic era and finish with the post–World War II period.[28] The exposition tries to cover the tremendous long-term period: from mentioning Paleolithic era (through ancient statues), ethnographical part (through clothes and everyday life elements) to the Ottoman period, Russian Empire collaboration, and finally, part of war and postwar period. The Podgorica City Museum is the only museum in the city that mentions the Yugoslavian period. This two-story building, founded in 1950, is located in close vicinity to the center and looks as being properly preserved.

The socialist time is mentioned in the context of Tito's visit to Podgorica after World War II. These two events (end of the war and Tito's arrival) are selectively chosen as such, which might represent the key event or the fundamental atmosphere of city history in the middle of the twentieth

---

[28] http://museu.ms/museum/172/city-museum-of-podgorica

century. The main visual method is representation of photos, accompanied by information plaques.

The space given to the period of the second part of the twentieth century is small. If one analyzes the displayed photos, one might notice the serious damage the city suffered during World War II. One will understand this message through the photos with such titles "Citizens of Podgorica in a Refugee Camp," "Collapse of the Occupiers Troops 1944," and "Plan of the Dropped Bombs on Podgorica." The message is supported by the short description representing information for the whole block. There it is also stated that the city was damaged during the war. Going forward, from those several photos showing a period of war, one will see the next period—the post–World War II period. It is shown as a new epoch with the spirit of collectivity, which is displayed through the photos of brigades that rebuild the city (the plaque "Communists at hard labor" and "Sports and workers association ZORA") (Photo 5.20). After stand with photos showing bombed Podgorica is located, then several photos showing the postwar urban reconstructions, the view of the reconstructed city, and finally the exposition is finished with the photo of Tito and Blazo Jovanovic waving people who surround them from their open car in the streets of Titograd. Taking into consideration the entire amount of presented photos, one may see the visible priority of main events and their connotation as it was constructed by the creation of the exhibition. The key aspects in understanding the representation of Yugoslav period are shown through the last stand with two plaques: "Postwar Podgorica" and "Tito and Blaze Jovanovic." It forms the vision of Yugoslavia as the new era. Era, associated with active construction of the city and era of visible collectivity. The previous periods are presented through the things (instance of a sword, a pitcher), landscapes, and "typical" people of the time (portraits). The Yugoslav period has the new dimension of visual representation—the sense of collectivity. Such a feeling is expressed through the display of the collective work, for instance, photo that depicts people that are digging or doing physical exercises together. The second characteristic of representation of a given period is the personification of the period through Tito Broz candidature. Both elements construct the vision of Yugoslavia as the period of collective productivity and happiness. I argue that the image of productivity is formed through the visual image of photos showing intensive dynamic activity of the city population. The second image, "happiness," is built through the selection of photos where people and the leader are smiling and having mutual sympathy.

Photo 5.20: Podgorica City Museum, Podgorica, December 2013

History Museum, Cetinje

All of the museums located in the city, except two (Museum of the Cetinje Monastery and Electric Industry Museum) function as a part of the National Museum of Montenegro institution. The given institution comprises of the State Museum, "Petar Petrovic Njegoš" Museum, Ethnographic Museum, History Museum, and Art Museum. Cetinje is also a home city of central archive, library, national theater, and official residence of the Montenegrin president called the "Blue Palace." All of those buildings create the image of the city as the cultural and heritage capital.

All of the given museums had good conditions, proper temperature regime and light, and information in several languages. However, none of them presented the Yugoslavian period. They were transmitting either the nineteenth-century showpieces and creating the ethnographic exhibition of the "traditional life" in Montenegro or the artefacts and history of the country through the royal family history. The third spectrum is the religious objects representing the orthodox heritage. The role of the royal dynasty has significant place and is confirmed by such statement from the official National Museum of Montenegro website: "the museum departments dedicated to particular persons—Prince-Bishop and writer Petar II Petrovic Njegoš and the last Montenegrin King Nikola I Petrovic Njegoš—have special appeal."[29]

The History Museum is the largest building compared to other departments spread throughout Cetinje. Its frames have to include the history of the second half of the twentieth century, but at the moment of observation (November 2013), the last exhibition was representing the beginning of the twentieth century. The period of World War II and socialist Yugoslavia was not available, and according to the words of staff, it is on the museum's schedule to create the exhibition dedicated to Yugoslavian period. Thereby, due to the absence of the given period in the museums, it is problematic to give any reasonable characteristic of the research period.

However, in order to create at least some image on the attitude toward the recent past in the museum space, we made a conversation with the museum guide. I would claim that the positive attitude, which we saw at the City Museum through the photos, responds to the imagination of Yugoslavia which the staff have. When I asked what her personal perception of the Yugoslav times was, we received the answer based on the comparison of the current independent period and past times, with favor to the Yugoslavian period. The main logic could be reduced to the idea that Montenegro, being small in territory and resources, needs partners. The Yugoslavian times were understood by the guide, through the peaceful international friendship of the ex-Yugoslavian nations with each other ("We lived together in friendship. We didn't need visas .... It was a happy period").

Apart from the respondents' positive attitudes toward the past, we also observed the visual details. Thus, walking through Cetinje, we found a

---

29 http://www.mnmuseum.org/Index_e.html

private house with the Yugoslavian flag hanging on it. Moreover, coming closer, we have seen Tito Broz' statues and photos hanging on the side wall of the patio (Photo 5.21). On the left side of the yard the wet clothes were drying, which means that the place was residential. Over the entrance door we found a signboard: "Klub Jugonostalgicara Josip Broz Tito" (Josip Broz Tito Yugo-nostalgic Club) (Photo 5.22).

Photo 5.21: Yugo-nostalgic club and private house, Cetinje, December 2013

The third thing that I noticed was the common selling practice in Montenegro to use the car as a showcase and to sell some small stuff there. Usually, vendors were selling different calendars, stationery, and candles. Systematically, we have seen calendars with Tito on them. Tito's image was included in the row with other popular objects: small icons and calendars with naked women and nature (Photo 5.23).

Photo 5.22: Yugo-nostalgic club and private house, Cetinje, December 2013

Photo 5.23: Vendors' assortment, Podgorica, December 2013

Conclusions

The absence of the Yugoslavian period is visible also in the case of Montenegrin museums. The given institutions have shown that the interpretation of the pasthas not been developed; but based on our analysis of public space and dialogue with the staff of both museums, we would presume that museum politics toward the recent past will emerge soon in the space of museums, and the main focus would be given to the integrative aspects of the Yugoslavian life. The modernization and the urban constructions could become the general line of the visual museum discourse. I have shown on the example of Podgorica Museum, where the socialist period is mentioned in the new dimension of visual representation that is used when describing the given period—the sense of collectivity and the personification of the period by Tito Broz candidature. These two elements construct the vision of Yugoslavia as the period of collective productivity and happiness and form it through the visual image of photos showing intensive dynamic activity of the city population.

The presence of the same political party in power since the beginning of 1990s, the Democratic Party of Socialists that is the direct successor of the Yugoslav Communist Party, allows us to think that one should not expect significant transformations in the museum politics toward the past in the near future. The integration in the EU is the primary focus of the contemporary Montenegrin political strategy and, therefore, museums would have to balance between construction of the well-being of the past, which responds to the feelings of the majority of the population and creation of the historical continuity and logical development in the frames of European history and future.

The main hypothesis that we had was confirmed. We stated that the socialist period would be represented through the narrative of "brotherhood and unity" and the 1980s would be excluded from the exhibition. The vision with such connotation is available, but in a very reduced version, that we have described above.

5.4 Bosnia and Herzegovina

The memory landscape in Bosnia and Herzegovina has one very important characteristic: it consists of three main official narratives, which coexist, compete and are pronounced by fragmentation. Usually, there exists the dominant national narrative, even though it could be contested inside the country; but BiH, due to the constitutional legitimation of the three constituent ethnicities, has the unique coexistence and ongoing competition of three official memory narratives and ethno-national identity constructions (Moll 2013 3). Bosnian Serb nationalism is focused on Republika Srpska legitimation and contests the existence of BiH. Bosniak nationalism identifies itself with the country and from their side contest existence of Republika Srpska. The third type—Bosnian Croat nationalism—advocates the need to have its own entity at the state level and emphasize their outnumbered strength by the Bosniak majority in the Federation (Moll 2013, 2). Such entities have created and maintained different memory politics, which was analyzed by Moll (2012), who shows the differences in selecting official events for celebration or commemoration that are producing three different historical narratives in the country.

All three nationalism memories have similar elements—accentuation on the war period by the glorification of its own ethnicity together with its victimization. One pattern includes the glorification of one's own battles and soldiers combined with a strong emphasis on one's own victimhood, together with demonization of the other. Another common pattern is the denial of the "dark sides" of the ethnic group to which one belongs (Ramet 2007). The second important pattern is the reference to World War II and Partisans' antifascist legacy. Through the Partisan movement, the continuity with the wars of the 1990s is established (Kuljic 2010, 85—115). The wars of 1992–95 are seen by Bosniaks and Serbs as fascist aggression, but the role of fascists is played by another. Thus, both of them celebrate anniversary dates linked to Partisan battles, but different battles and dates are chosen (Moll 2013, 6). Additionally, Bosniaks have a special focus on the crimes committed by Chetniks in eastern Bosnia between 1941 and 1945, that is often presented as genocide (Moll 2013). At the same time, Bosnian Serbs heavily use the discourse of the Partisan movement with its application in the 1990s, while "the monuments to Serb victims of 1992–1995 are often placed in the vicinity of Partisan monuments or the latter are modified with the addition of the Serb flag or Orthodox symbols" (Moll 2013, 9). The Bosnian Croatian nationalism is based on strong anti-Yugoslav and anti-Partisan memories, with fixation of such memories by the erection of monuments dedicated to the Croat as the victims of the partisans (Moll 2013).

In addition to the three ethno-narratives presented, which are translated through the political actors, the anti-nationalism narrative is the fourth dimension. Its main actor in the political field is the Social Democrat Party, the former communist party whose main historical reference is "Tito's Yugoslavia in general and the antifascist struggle of the Second World War in particular" (Moll 2013, 13). The Yugo-nostalgia, as the background of this discourse, has support in society among diverse groups of population of different age, gender, and ethnic origins. An illustration of such attitudes may be the case from the recent protest, which took place in Sarajevo in 2009 when the main street "Maršal Tito street" were planning to change into "Alija Izetbegović street." The public revolt was organized by the Social Democrats and Yugo-nostalgic organization that joined them and 24,000 people who signed the petition to preserve the old name (Velikonja 2013, 364).

Due to the coexistence of the complex palette of history narrative relations in BiH, the observations of national museums might be understood as an attempt to analyze only the official representation of history.

At the time of my field trip (autumn 2013), Bosnia and Herzegovina had a population census: the first since 1991, the first in the last 22 years, and the first census after the war.[30] The issue was highly politicized (Velikonja 2013, 364). The religious institutions took an active role in the promotion of the "proper" identity of all three main religious movements: Orthodoxy, Islam, and Catholicism.[31]

---

[30] http://www.reuters.com/article/2013/09/27/us-bosnia-census-idUSBRE98Q0DT20130927

[31] Aija Kuge, Tri voprosa bosnihskoj vlasti (Айя Куге, Три вопроса боснийской власти), Radio Liberty, October 15, 2013, http://www.svoboda.org/content/article/25137085.html

I visited after the census took place, but some of the billboards were still reminding about the ethnic majority that had lived in the area where the bus took us. The title promoted "traditional values": "I'm Serbian, the citizen of the Serbian Republic, I like Orthodoxy and I talk Serbian" (Ja cam СРБИН, државьянин РЕПУБКИКЕ СРПСКЕ, ПРАВОСЛАВЉЕ волим, СРПСКИ зборим) (Photo 5.24). The appeal to the ethnic identification and expected religious correspondence remain an operative tool for electoral mobilization.

Photo 5.24: Census 2013 billboard, Sarajevo suburb, December 2013

By the time I arrived at the city center, it met me with the other indicator of actual competing memory—the Islamic tombs covered the majority of park areas all through the city center. Some of them were old, but the majority appeared after the Siege of Sarajevo period. The death became part of the landscape, not of that classical one: the pastoral of peaceful village where time and death have its time, but of the silent genocide of own population. Pedestrians peacefully walk their dogs nearby, the shopping malls promote new collections of status attributes, drivers hurry—life goes on.

Traditionally, the graves are fenced but not in Sarajevo. Here, they are public, without any barrier, which would create the imagined border between the daily life and sacral space (Photos 5.25 and 5.26). The publicity of the death creates its totality and interweaves it with the everyday life landscape. This makes the death trivial. And making the death trivial makes the place horrible, which means making the place out of order, out of our stability.

Not surprisingly, the most recent topic to present is the period between 1992 and 1995. The same period is represented both in the Historical Museum of Bosnia and Herzegovina and in city center galleries. Special tours are organized to the "Tunnel of Hope" museum, the tunnel that connected Sarajevo citizens with the airport—the only possible way to escape or to receive aid from the world.

Photo 5.25: Public park, Sarajevo, December 2013

Photo 5.26: Public park, Sarajevo, December 2013

The National Museum of Bosnia and Herzegovina

The state museums are located at the "new" center of the city, very close to the railway and bus station and embassies. They are located at a 20-minute walking distance from the main attraction of the city—the Old town and museums that are located there (City Museum, Jewish Museum, mosque, galleries). This may have an influence on the number of visitors and the level of priority of these buildings to be reconstructed.

The National Museum of Bosnia and Herzegovina in Sarajevo is the oldest museum institution in the country, founded in 1888 at the time of the Austrian-Hungarian Empire (Lozic 2011, 75). During the socialist period, it was transformed into the museum of the revolution with the concentration on the "brotherhood and unity" and working-class focus paradigm. After 1992, the war period brought damages to four buildings of the museum and it was closed until the end of the siege. Since 1995, it has been a beneficiary of international financial aid as a significant cultural institution (Lozic 2011, 78). However, it has been closed since October 2012 for an indefinite period because of the lack of financial support. Being "the main agents in the museological presentation and mediation of history,"

(Lozic 2011, 72) it puts some light on the crisis situation within the museum politics.

In the postwar Bosnia, all the religious institutions were issued to be reconstructed. By implementing such a strategy, the government was trying to demonstrate the multicultural nature of the country. Thus, by the support of UNESCO and different states, some churches and mosques were reconstructed. The museum object—Haggadah—also became part of the non-museum discourses (Hajdarpasic 2008, 113). This object belonged to the Sephardic Jewish family, who sold it to the museum. For a long period, it was kept in the warehouses, but after the end of war conflict of 1990s, the object became the core of the new exposition. The manuscript started to symbolize the political tolerance and the inclusive character of the country. The objects became an instrument to be exploited by the politicians for populist rhetoric because it was easier to extrapolate the vision of ethnic tolerance to the neutral side that was not involved in the conflict (Hajdarpasic 2008, 116). The objects embodied the images of nationalism with a multicultural face and postnationalism (Ostow 2008, 7). "In Bosnian's national museum, the 'rescued' Sarajevo Haggadah is featured as a display of the moral integrity of Bosnian nation" (Ostow 2008, 9). However, Ostow correctly remarks that through the Haggadah, the multiculturalism was reduced to the issue of "multiconfessionalism" (Ostow 2008, 10).

The example of the Haggadah illustrates how historical objects could easily receive new meanings and political connotations and be used in different discourses. While it was the key object of the museum and a good example of the constructive nature of the historical exhibitions, we have mentioned it. The next step would be the description of another history museum.

The Historical Museum of Bosnia and Herzegovina

The museum was founded in 1945 and served as an institution predominantly highlighting the liberation movement of the World War II period (Makaš 2012, 5). The former title "The Museum of National Liberation in

Sarajevo" confirms the notion. The museum did not have a permanent location until 1963, when the building constructed particularly for the museum purposes was opened. After several years in 1967, its title was changed to the Museum of Revolution of Bosnia and Herzegovina. Finally, in 1993, together with the transformation of the museum's paradigm, the given institution received its current name (Lozic 2011, 84).

The Historical Museum of Bosnia and Herzegovina is a two-story building at a good location but is in poor condition (Photo 5.27). There were no guides or audio-guides available, but the plaques were made in both Bosnian language and English. The security guard cum cashier told me that they don't have English guide and that the average number of visitors is approximately 40 per day.

Photo 5.27: The Historical Museum of Bosnia and Herzegovina, Sarajevo, December 2013

At the moment of observation, there were three expositions available. Two of them were located on the second floor and one, the least visited, on the first. The second floor was divided into two exhibition rooms: each for separate exposition. The most visited one was, as we mentioned before, the "Besieged of Sarajevo." The plaques were made in English and in Bosnian.

At the entrance to the exhibition, there was information written on a paper warning visitors about disturbing content and, therefore, visitors have to decide on their own responsibility if they would like to join in. The exposition begins with information about the roots of war. In this regard, Yugoslavia is referred to Serbia and Montenegro in conjunction with its desire to create the Greater Serbia. The plaque answers the question of the reasons for having war:

> "The causes of the aggression against Bosnia and Herzegovina cannot be separated from the causes that led from the breaking up of the Yugoslavia. One of the major causes therefore was the incapacity and unpreparedness for democratic changes. The historical dream of Greater Serbia was presented as a solution to the democratization of the former SFRY. Instead of facing the essential issues of democratic changes, which would rely on the parliamentary democracy, a market economy, with full respect of human rights, the 'Serbia question' was presented. A clash of totalitarianism and democracy ended in the aggression against Bosnia and Herzegovina."

Hence, from this plaque we see that Yugoslavia is characterized as a non-democratic union with unprepared mechanisms for economic and political changes. I would like to mention that the question of the break-up and its representations in different museums needs very careful research for further scientific purposes. In the given research, I focus only on the interpretation of the Yugoslav period and would mention the next stand dealing with it.

On it we see a photo of the protest; in the middle of the crowd, a large picture of Tito is visible (Photo 5.28). The explanation under the stand says that it is dedicated to the "peaceful rally in front of the BiH Parliament, 4 April 1994." It's very important to notice the link between the picture and the characteristics of it. We see the word "peaceful demonstration" and we see Tito's portrait as the representative of such division. Yugoslavia was called undemocratic, but Tito was shown as the leader of the peaceful country. Yugoslavia is peaceful and undemocratic—that's what we can understand from the texts if we compare them. Perhaps, one should also divide two different Yugoslav images: Tito's Yugoslavia and state after his death. The second one is associated with Serbian rule, even though Slobodan Milosevic, who came to power in the late eighties, is not mentioned at those stands which we've analyzed.

Photo 5.28: Temporal exhibition, the Historical Museum of Bosnia and Herzegovina, Sarajevo, December 2013

The period of the siege and the representation of The Hague tribunal would be skipped, but I would mention that the newest stands are used while representing the exposition dedicated to the tribunal. The central part of the room is used under the representation of the "20 years of the international justice, 1993–2013." It answers the following question: why and when the tribunal was open? It gives some statistics on the numbers of crimes made during the war. It shows three stories made by three victims of Albanian, Bosniak, and Bosnian Serb origins, who survived. The plasma display is located at this exposition, but during our visit it was not working.

From its reorientation in 1993, the museum also serves as "a memorial space of the most recent war" (Lozic 2011, 85) and had a lot of expositions about the recent war period (Ibid.).

The second exposition is an international photo project called "One Day in the World" and it doesn't have any links to the Yugoslav presentation.

To understand better the given period, let's move outside the museum in its backyard. First, what we shall notice there is the monument of Tito covered with yellow ribbons crosswise. When entering the museum, one sees the picture with the same statue of Tito in ribbons and some other statues or other artefacts from different museums.. All of them are covered with similar yellow ribbons with the following inscription on each: "Culture shut down." This collective action of putting ribbons and clothing for one day in museums was inspired by the solidarity day with the National Museum; another museum located at, approximately, 30 meters from the observed museum has been closed for almost a year. The aim of the action is to "highlight the crisis of cultural institutions in Bosnia and Herzegovina," where one is already closed and others are at the risk of having the same future. The action is described on the Cultureshutdown.net web page.

Returning to the monument of Tito in the yard, we also notice military equipment displayed as museum showpieces (Photo 5.29). Children play with them. Each piece has a plaque. On the left side of the museum building, in the ground floor, a Yugo-nostalgic café-bar is located (Photo 5.30). Its nostalgic essence was described by Makaš (2012, 6) who referred to it as a constant representative of the Yugo-nostalgia and a popular place. The entrance is decorated with the poster that reminds us about May 25—the Day of the Youth (25. Maj-Dan Mladosti). The other poster states: We are Tito's (Mi smo Titovi). The bar was full of young people when I visited it. The time was around 2 p.m. and it was the middle of the week. The entrance walls were painted in red color and the old photos and pictures were hanging on them. All of them were showing the Yugoslavian period: Partisans on the tanks, big street at the time of the parade with a picture of Tito in the middle of the street wall, a compilation of photos of Tito.

Photo 5.29: Yard, the Historical Museum of Bosnia and Herzegovina, Sarajevo, December 2013

Photo 5.30: Tito-nostalgic pub, the Historical Museum of Bosnia and Herzegovina, Sarajevo, December 2013

The interior met us with typical Tito/Yugo-nostalgic entourage: posters of Marshall Tito during different international visits, pictures, photos related to Yugoslavian time, slogans: "Death to Fascism. Freedom to the people" (Smrt fašizmu. Svoboda narodu) glued to the wall, rifles, and many other elements that make the space breathe with the special spirit of socialism with common goals. Such place is an illustration of the visible trend related to Yugo-nostalgic consumerism. As it was shown by Velikonja (2013), in BiH, nostalgia is not only a popular political position but also a successful commercial product. Our observations give similar results. Thus, in the museum shop, the products related to Yugoslav topics, such as T-shirts with Tito's image on it, were the most presented products (Photo 5.31). The availability of the Yugo-nostalgic pub in the walls of the museum is another argument.

Photo 5.31: Museum shop, the Historical Museum of Bosnia and Herzegovina, Sarajevo, December 2013

If one visits the official Web site of the museum, one will also find a positive reference to Yugoslavia, even though it has just a slight mention of it. Thus, the online page of the museum offers a visual tour of the ongoing exhibition called "The Sarajevo Survival Tools" that represents the objects used by the citizens during the 1992–96 siege of the city. The virtual tour was developed by the students from e-Faculty of Electrical Engineering

Sarajevo (ETF). It starts with several minute video that may be perceived as an introduction to the exhibition. It describes the idea of the exhibition and provides the visitor with a particular vision of Sarajevo's prewar past. First, the video describes the history of Sarajevo through the concept of coexistence of religious diversity and plural identities that accompanied Sarajevo's urban life through the centuries before 1992. The second Yugoslavia is mentioned through inscription into the concept of reaching plurality—the Winter Olympic Games and continues the narration of multicultural peaceful coexistence. The event is used as a highly important element for constructing the official memory narrative (Moll 2013, 5). A part of the video message is as follows: "Sarajevo is the only city in Europe where mosques, synagogues, Eastern Orthodox and Roman Catholic churches stand so close to each other .... The modern history of the city was marked by the 1984 Winter Olympic Games when Sarajevo had an opportunity to show its authentic and unique hospitality. The Siege of Sarajevo started."[32]

The museum heritage in Sarajevo is in an ambivalent situation. There are some of the museums that have a high enough subsidy from the government to function well. Among them we could call "Museum of the city of Sarajevo," "Jewish museum," "Tunnel of Hope museum" and the "Memorial Gallery 11/07/95" (presenting photo documents from the genocide camps). The national historical museum was in worse condition compared to the listed cultural objects. It is difficult to find regularities for the selectivity of funding museums. Neither the territorial principle nor the topic has fully answered the question. One thing is correct: the war period is the most visible at Sarajevo. The Memorial Gallery "11/07/95," which is located at the city center, at the Old Center (Old Center—the top touristic destination in Sarajevo) has the most expensive entrance fee and, perhaps, has the best equipment and contemporary view. The other war-related museum is located in the peripheral area, among the suburban private houses, close to the airport. The most common way to reach it is to come by taxi. It is in a good condition, is not big, and is a famous tourist destination. It has received additional popularity because of a few celebrities,

32 Sarajevo Survival Tools, video tour, http://h.etf.unsa.ba/srp/vmuzej/voda-e.htm

such as John Travolta, Orlando Bloom, Morgan Freeman, and Kevin Spacey, who have visited it once.

The museum of the city of Sarajevo also duplicates the Siege of Sarajevo. Returning to the analyzed historical museum and, as described earlier, seeing that it is also involved in the representation of the war issue, its location is not at the periphery of the city. Nevertheless, these two factors did not help much to receive good subsidy for the reconstruction of the building, which the museum needs.

I think the reason for weak functioning lies not only in the economic reasons, even though it is true, but the building contains more space than those museums from the list. The other reason is the lack of necessity to make new expositions. Seems it is because the dominant issue (the siege) is represented and it is enough to justify the maintenance of the building. The dominant national narrative is constructed by fixation of the victimization discourses. The violence and atrocities, when presented, transmit not only the function of remembrance but a branch of subordinate functions used in different fields. On the political level, which is closely linked to the ideological one, the governance identifies the topping argument for its existence. In other words, any government needs the key event in history, which would be the leitmotif of their causation. There has to exist always the ideological reason produced by the government, which augments the legitimacy of the regime. A core reason is taken from the actualized historical period and transmitted through different channels such as media, educational programs, and, of course, museums.

The economic reasons are also closely related to politics: with the limited budget, there has to be chosen the most key events to be represented. The official site of the museum provides the visitor with the brief history of the museum and also mentions the absence of the professionals as an important aspect of the current condition of the museum: "Today, museum works in a very difficult material situation, especially has the problem with lack of professional staff."[33]

---

[33] The Historical Museum of BiH, website, http://www.muzej.ba/index.php?lang=en&sel=2

In such a situation, the Yugoslav period is wiped off from the exhibitions due to economic reasons (weak funding) and because it makes no point for the legitimization of the current government. Yugoslavia (as it is mentioned) comes only as a mechanism to prove statements regarding the most recent and dramatic past (1992–1995).

Conclusions

When analyzing Bosnia and Herzegovina, one need to remember the existence of the complex political division in the country, which consists basically of three main official ethnic narratives, which coexist, compete and are pronounced by fragmentation through the country. Due to the constitutional legitimation of the three constituent ethnicities, Bosniaks, Croats, and Serbs, the Bosnian case requires additional explanations and serious research in order to understand the ethno-national identity constructions which is present in the country. Bosnian Serb nationalism, which is focused on Republika Srpska legitimation, contests the existence of BiH; Bosniaks nationalism identifies itself with the country and contest existence of Republika Srpska; Bosnian Croat nationalism advocates the need to have its own entity on the state level and emphasize their strength by the Bosniak majority in the Federation (Moll 2012, 2). The political division is reflected through the museum spaces in the form of maintenances of the different memory politics. The way of selecting official events for celebration or commemoration, referring to different aspects of the (un)common past produces three different historical narratives in the country. However, all three of them have a similarity—they make accents on the recent war period by the glorification of its own ethnicity together with strong emphasis on one's own victimhood and with demonization of the other.

The analysis has shown the existence of different levels of dealing with the socialist past. The Historical Museum period of Yugoslavia is mentioned in conjunction with the upcoming siege and war. Since reorientation of the museums in the early 1990s, it serves as "a memorial space of the most recent war" (Lozic 2011, 85).

Yugoslavia is characterized through the economic and political problems of 1980s as a nondemocratic union with unprepared mechanisms for economic and political changes, but at the same time as a peaceful period of living. Generally, a dominant trend is visible in the politics of memory in Sarajevo—the representation of the traumatic past. If the national museums are in a poor condition and require general restoration of the premises, there are other types of museum spaces visibly contrasting with them. Just to mention "Tunnel of Hope museum" and the "Memorial Gallery 11/07/95" (presenting photos from the Srebrenica genocide).

As mentioned before, the representation of the Yugoslavian period consists of different layers and some of them confirms its actuality. We have called one of such layers commercial initiative.

This was visible through the products which the historical museum's shop was offering. The majority of goods were related to the "peaceful Yugoslavian imagination" like portraits of Tito in a frame and similar-in-content things. Another place with a similar connotation was the Yugo-nostalgic café-bar located in the ground floor of the museum, which we have described in our research.

In general, the proposed hypotheses were confirmed during the visual analysis. However, the first part of the hypothesis that Yugoslavia will be divided into two opposing periods, before Tito's death and after, was not possible to confirm or reject, while the period before 1980s was not the issue of the exhibition. The second and the third hypotheses were correct: Yugoslavia of the 1980s was represented through the issue of Serbian nationalism and together with the economic factors have led to the dramatic situation of the 1990s. The discovered line to focus on the last decade of the 1980s at the researched museum confirms the general line of memory politics in Bosnia and Herzegovina, with the center in Sarajevo, to focus on the period of the recent dramatic past. The Siege of Sarajevo and Srebrenica became the visual representation of the traumatic past.

5.5 Croatia

The beginning of the 1990s was marked by a historical revisionism tendency. The streets and squares were receiving new names. The important points of symbolic identification of the socialist past were massively changed with identifiers of national narratives. Thus, streets with Partisan names transformed into names from the earlier Croatian history.[34] The square which was called the "Fascism Victims Square" during the second Yugoslavia was renamed into the "Square of great Croats" and existed in such form until 2000 (Stanić 2009). Another important shift was related to commemoration practices dedicated to the World War II period. If during Yugoslavian period, Jasenovas, the concentration camp where under the protectorate of Ustashas the mass crimes were committed, it was the main commemoration place. In the early 1990s, it was substituted to the concurrent memory of commemorations in Bleiberg, Austrian town, where in May 1945, Partisans killed thousands of fleeing Croats (Ustashas, soldiers, civilians) (Moll 2013, 11). The relativization of Ustashas crimes with accentuation on Partisan crimes became the characteristic visible in history books prepared for schools (Cvijic 2008, 716). With the change of political forces in 2000, the process of revisionism was reduced. The Square mentioned before received its socialist name[35] and the commemoration of Jasenovac became the tradition of state political elites again (Ibid.).

How the recent history is represented in contemporary Zagreb will be shown in the following part.

There are two main historical museums in Zagreb: the Croatian History Museum and the Zagreb City Museum. Both of them are located close to each other in the most expensive area of the city near the governmental institutions of power.

First of all, I've visited the Croatian History Museum as the most relevant place for comparison, but the content of the exhibition "Gnalić—Treasure

---

[34] V techeniye 90-kh godov gosudarstvennyye prazdniki chasto menyalis'(in Russian), Radio Liberty, December 18, 2012, http://www.svoboda.org/content/backgrounderfullpage/24801326.html

[35] Ibid.

of a 16th century sunken ship" was irrelevant for the topic of my research. It was the only exhibition taking place at the moment of observation. Even though the museum is located at a large territory of several floors, only part of it is used for museum purposes. The limitations of the space for representations force the organizers to make all exhibitions on the temporal basis and only in a singular number during each period. The given exhibition presents artefacts, which were found on the wrecks in Croatia.

It would be useful to mention that the state of visualization is of high level. First of all, the placement is organized with the required temperature regime, all equipment looks new, plaques are made in both Croatian and English languages.

During one of my previous visits in 2012, there was a temporal exhibition dedicated to the armed conflict/war in Croatia at the 1990s between Serbian actors and Croatia—the Homeland War. The accent was made on two regions: Vukovar and Osjek. That exhibition definitely needs special attention, but while our topic is not related to the disintegration we shall avoid any descriptions on it. The only thing, which we would mention and which might be useful for understanding the mood of the population, is the fact that the given exposition had the highest number of visitors during the last decade. The museum guide mentioned that the number of locals, who came to visit the exhibition, was higher compared to any other exhibition before and after it. The main reason, in the guide's words, is its contemporaneity and actuality, "because it is about the people who are still alive."

The museum is "sitting on its suitcases" since 1956 and waiting for relocation to its own building. This fact explains the situation with limited exposition spaces. One of the guides mentioned: "We have around 300,000 items at the museum fund ... from which we have shown third part of them ... during the last 50 years." If the final relocation takes place during this year, there would be plans to prepare a permanent exhibition on contemporary history of Croatia with the inclusion of Yugoslav period and time of Croatian independence.

It would be useful to mention the number of visitors per year: 12,000–15,000; two thirds of the visitors are tourists.

The Zagreb City Museum

The museum is located at a few minutes' walk from the previously described museum; it is a well-organized, large-scale space with exhibitions dealing with the history from prehistorical period up to the contemporary world. The disintegration of Yugoslavia is the home stretch of the exhibited materials. The last room in the whole museum is demonstrating the latest 1980s and beginning of the 1990s with the inclusion of the wars in Croatia. But let's start our observation from the point when Yugoslavia was first mentioned—World War II.

We'll find Ante Pavelic's picture, coat of arms of the war period of the Independent State of Croatia, and several posters from that time. The description, which hangs near clarifies the crimes made by the Ustasha to several main groups: ethnic group (such as Serbs and Jews) and ideological adversary (such as communist Partisans). The words to describe the Ustasha regime are "the reign of terror," the Partisans' "resistance movement." Such an interpretation of Ustasha's role as clear Nazi collaborants and criminals is the product of the early 2000 politics when a country has chosen the liberal and more leftist government in the elections which took place soon after Tujman's death (Ramet 2010, 273). The clear ideological direction toward European integration and movement toward the democratization process was developing together with the return to the more balanced revision of the "revisioned history" in the 1990s, when Ustasha movement was strongly relativized (Cvijic 2008, 716). As mentioned in one of the previous chapters, in the contemporary politics of commemoration in Croatia, sufficient role is given to regular commemorating of the liberation of the Jasenovac concentration camp (Cvijic 2008, 720). The importance of the given place as a symbolic articulation is reproduced in the history books and, as I have found out, also in museums.

Close to the stand, one will find the column with the quote of Tito's speeches about the braveness of women, who participated in the Partisan movement. From the other side of the same column, there is a short documentary showing the replacement of the monument of Josip Jelacic to the huge, tasteless Red soldier monument in the main square of Zagreb. The figure of Josip Jelacic is the symbol of Croatian independence, and it can be noted that after receiving independence, the monument of the soldier was removed back to the identically important Ban of Croatia.

The description of this column shows the most important characteristics, balanced reflexivity, while both regimes the Ustasha and Socialists are presented not as unicolorous but with the demonstrative visualization of the regime's spirit. The triumph of the winner is combined with the ideological restrictions which it brings.

The second characteristic of the exposition after being critical is the concentration on the cultural aspects of the Yugoslav period. This will be clear if we go ahead and briefly list other stands at the room. We'll find here stand showing two female types of clothes: some ethnic or rural clothes and city clothes (Photo 5.32). Moreover, the mannequin in the urban clothes symbolizes the development of a socialistically successful new type of women. The plaque is telling the story of Vesna Kinic Murtic, the hairdresser, who won different international honors during the competitions for her talent.

Photo 5.32: Zagreb City Museum, Zagreb, December 2013

The walls are decorated with posters from the cultural events: music events, concerts, film festivals (Photo 5.33).

After leaving this room, one needs to go to the floor above, where several more rooms and the hall are related to the Yugoslav period representations. The hall is also decorated with different posters, which continue the cultural approach of previous exposition: numerous concerts, festivals, exhibitions, and other cultural events taking place in Zagreb are placed here. The only new element at the end of the hall are the posters of political parties that arose in the late 1980s and the early 1990s in Croatia.

Photo 5.33: Zagreb City Museum, Zagreb, December 2013

The first room of the two is represents the famous Zagreb school of animated film (Photo 5.34). The central element of the exposition is the Oscar-winning animated short film "Surogat" created by Dušan Vukotić, which is screened on the TV located in the room.

Photo 5.34: Zagreb City Museum, Zagreb, December 2013

The next room is also film oriented but in different meaning. If the cartoon was the subject of the exposition, here the documentary is the object of representation of the certain period—disintegration of Yugoslavia. The decoration of the room is simple—brick walls with several photos on it. The photos are showing representatives of the government together with religious leaders standing in front of the Croatian flag; Pope John Paul II arrival to Zagreb; tank (Photo 5.35). From these posters it is visible, how the events are selected to construct the traditional national identity which does not truly recognize multiculturalism: independence, Catholicism, war. Three main elements are made simple and gives a clear message—the true Croat is of Catholic origin who will fight for his or her independence.

Photo 5.35: Zagreb City Museum, Zagreb, December 2013

To fix our idea and to find more evidences for our conclusions we shall itemize what is shown in the film. First of all, our research title is of the crucial importance: Yugoslavia—A Prison of Nations.

So, what is proposed?

1. Concert of the rock band "Prljavo Kazaliste"
2. Confrontation of football fans during the football match "Dinamo-Crnvena Zvezda" in 1989 year in Zagreb
3. Winning of the elections by Franjo Tuđman
4. Removal of Yugoslav flag to the Croatian
5. Restoration of the monument to Josip Jelacic
6. Croatian protests at the areas close to Serbian borders
7. Chronicles of armed conflict
8. Bombing of Zagreb's TV tower
9. Arrival of Pope John Paul II
10. Chronicles from 1995
11. Return of the soldiers to Zagreb

What kind of image of Yugoslavia does this film give? Does the film emphasize visible reasons why Yugoslavia is called a prison of nations? In my opinion, the film doesn't give the unequivocal answer. On the one hand, it is clearly stated that the ethical clashes between Croats and Serbs existed before the collapse, but the independence, following the logic, brought the apogee of the ethical conflicts. The image of Yugoslavia is less uniquely negative if we look to the previous room, where the product of the Yugoslav period—Zagreb animation received the highest recognition that Croatia ever had.

Conclusions

The historical revisionism that started in the 1990s with creation of anti-Yugoslav narrative in the form of substitution of the street names and monuments named in the socialist period to the historical periods of the earlier history was slowed in 2000 after Tuđman's death and some sufficient political transformations. Clear ideological direction toward European integration and movement toward the democratization process was developing together with creation of more balanced vision of the problematic pages of the past of the past. Since then, there has not been any serious transformations in the official collective memory. The analyzed museums go in line with the political vector.

The balanced reflexivity and attempts to present the history in a critical way created the space with the unicolorous. The triumph of the winner of fascism in the Balkans—the Partisans are combined with a demonstration of the ideological restrictions which the new regime brought.

The second characteristic of the exposition and its unique approach was the concentration on the cultural aspects of the Yugoslav period. This was illustrated by the case of the story of Vesna Kinic Murtic, the famous hairdresser, or the cartoon "Surogat" (Substitute) that received the Oscar, or the variety of posters with the concerts which took place in Zagreb.

Zagreb City Museum tried to make a balanced exhibition dedicated to the Yugoslav period, but when it came to analysis of the history of the 1990s, the classic narrative of cardinal victimization of the nation was used. It seems to me that such monosyllabic presentations are dealing with the late Yugoslavia even though it is not emphasized. The Sarajevo Museum could be understood from the same parallel, where the Siege of Sarajevo was interpreted as the reasons for having a background in Yugoslavia of the 1980s. However, if in Bosnian museum the economic reasons were emphasized, Croatian version has cultural background. The markers of national belonging are constructed through such indicators as religion, cultur (music and art legacy) and language. The hypotheses were rejected. The most unexpected aspect during our visual analysis was the absence of the Naken Island issue, especially because geographically it is located in Croatia. The second aspect unexpected for us was the absence of the reference to the Croatian Spring. Therefore, the actualizing of the maritime narrative was not the case of Zagreb museums and we would explain it by the general cultural specialization of the City Zagreb Museum where the analysis took place. The national history museum at the moment of observations had a lack of space and did not deal with the Yugolsavian or recent history. In order to analyze the dynamics of memory politics in the country, it is required to have an additional examination with inclusion of other cities into the analytical map of our research. Both Kumrovec and Naked Island might be included into the list together with the Vukovar, Osjek, and other relevant cities.

6 GENERAL CONCLUSIONS

Museums are rarely taken into focus by sociologists and political analysts; their role in constructing the social reality is usually underestimated or neglected. Such unappreciated role of state institutions created as the legitimized structure of the representation of the past, heritage, or culture is even more surprising at the time when their number is rapidly increasing and the role of science is becoming dominant. Museums "came to be widely regarded as modern scientific society's 'secular cathedrals,' 'guardians of shared history,' or 'storehouses for national treasures' " (Luke 2002, xiv). By having the power of secular significance, these institutions of memory have become "high-profile places for heated struggle over many exhibitions as sites for moralizing memorials, highly politicized polemics, and ritualized reflection" (Ibid.).

The transformations have accompanied museums from its creation in the late nineteenth century, being established as the cabinets of curiosity or simply a collection of strange, rare, and unique things, museums have become important actors with the main function "to display the public to itself, so that it was possible to see what it meant to be a model citizen" (Barrett 2011, 57). In a similar way, today museums are also viewed as disciplinary spaces in demonstrating the "true and correct" lived experience of citizenship and democracy. As the product of the modern society, museums were part of the state-engineered program of national public space construction, going in line with emergences of such public utilities as hospitals, transportation systems, libraries, universities, schools, and parks (Ibid.). Having the main function in preserving the important heritage, they were also involved in the creation of this value system based on selection of word-for-preservation element. Additionally, museums were the platform of educating the population and in such a role were maintaining the class order. The role of museums in maintaining the feeling of national belonging and common descent was noted by Benedict Anderson, who mentions these public institutions as the places of national imagination about itself. Museums continue to play the role of the visual representation of the nation for itself and in such role they were extremely interesting for our research. In such a role, museums inherited the important permanent self-characteristic— being a political object, but such a serious aspect of its existences as mentioned before is still often neglected in the political studies.

> "Indeed, most are shocked when they find truly heated political struggle at museums, and even then they do not take these conflicts seriously. In fact, museums rarely are regarded as affording rich opportunities for political analysis, and those that do exist are, all too often, consigned by professional prejudice to cultural studies departments at best or to the style sections of big urban newspapers at worst. I see this blindness in mainstream political science as a tragic flaw" (Luke 2002, xiii).

In this study, I aimed to change such neglection and to show how museums are creating, maintaining, and legitimizing a particular vision of the past and represent it as a verified history. The possibilities of comparison have allowed us to see the multiparadigmality of the interpretations arising from differences in the political agenda of the newly formed national states. I have taken into focus of analysis the same historical period consonant in each country—the Socialist Federal Republic of Yugoslavia, SFRY or as usually called second Yugoslavia or simply Yugoslavia.

The analysis of the national history museums of the former Yugoslavian republics has shown how socialist period is reflected in the state institutions responsible for representation of the past today. This research has shown very rich possibilities and differences in making accents created by each country. The types of narratives, ways of constructing the visibility of the same period, and the differences in connotations became a significant part of the analysis. The diversity of strategies of how the state and other political actors may influence on the material represented at the exposition, as well as the ways of political manipulations were presented at both parts of empirical analysis. The given study has confirmed the paradigmatic statement about the constructivist nature of the material represented as the history or as the past. The liquidity, flexibility, and possibility of accentuation on some aspects of the historical frames and oblivion of others were visible through the implementation of visual analysis at the ongoing exhibitions.

The essence of the given research can be presented concisely in the form of a table, where we summarize the main aspects of representation and existing trends for each country. It is shown below and is followed by the analysis provided for each national case.

Table 6.1: Summary of the visual representation by each country case

Country	Tendency on representation of Yugoslavia	Keywords	National mythological construct	Conditions of the museum
Macedonia*	"Repressive Yugoslavia"	Naked Island, repressions, control, crime	Antiquization	active role of the state: newly opened versus under oblivion
Kosovo	"lacunic time"	-	Ethnicization and European integration	Active role of the state through the European foundations; renovated
Bosnia and Herzegovina	"Reflection on the dissolution"	Growth of nationalism, economic stagnation, growing tensions, role of EU as a mediator	Victimization discourse	Not sufficient financial conditions; national museums are under oblivion. Exception is made for City Museum and galleries dealing with Siege Period and Srebrenica
Montenegro	"Yugoslavia as a positive glance"	Reconstructions of the post–World War II cities, urbanization	Not defined, elements of imperialism	Well equipped
Serbia*	"multivectorness and actualization: repressive versus glorified versus modernization"	Unfinished modernization, everyday life, dictator, leader, heritage, Naked Island, nostalgia, products, culture	Imperialism	Depends on the museum. National Museum is well equipped, part of MYH is well maintained (House of Flowers, Old Museum), other part needs more attention
Croatia	"Cultural determination over authoritarianism"	Modernization, film industry, fashion, Oscar, growth of Serbian nationalism, ethnic tensions	National discourse of independence	Well equipped, good conditions
Slovenia*	Authoritarian (might be transformed)	Red barons, Naked Island, repressions, economical problems, pollution, consumption	National discourse of independence	Well equipped, good conditions

*Conclusions are based on the research previously done. See: Zubkovych (2014, 2015a,b).

The ability to create particular meanings and to observe the formation of the counter-narratives was demonstrated in the cases of comparison of the historical exhibitions over the former Yugoslavia country's territory. From the nostalgia for the pre-socialist past to the accentuation of the disintegration discourse, from temporal oblivion to the total nostalgia, from balancing between critical reflections to the concentration on the cultural aspect of Yugoslavian history—these are the trends identified during our research. The political influence and the strategies of the state have been demonstrated as the permanent part of our research and became the most visible in the case of Macedonian museums.

Based on the analysis, I would suggest dividing countries into three categories according to the availability of different forms of nostalgic discourse. Thus, the dominant group consists of Slovenia, Serbia, Bosnia and Herzegovina, and Montenegro, which has shown either a commercial form of nostalgia and the individual or both of them. In this sense, the second category is the group with available anti-Yugoslav discourse or absence of its representation at all: Kosovo and Macedonia. Croatia, in the dimension of Zagreb museums forms the third category, while being neither nostalgic nor dogmatically anti-Yugoslav. According to the studies on nostalgia, the dissatisfaction with the current political, economic, or socioculturalsituation usually actualize this form of reflection. Another aspect is the vision of Yugoslavia as an unfinished modernization project and, therefore, from such perception the appeal to it as to the country where the modern values have originated might be the second explanation of nostalgia.

The third version is practicing nostalgia as a "retro." In such a case, Yugonostalgia is included in the consumption culture and does not have the complex meanings, while being just a simultaneous and easily substituted to any other "retro."

The absence or reduction of the narrative into the negative frames has also the possible explanations. As our study has shown, the selectivity and construction of the victimized discourse are typical for the cases where political intervention is most visible. Such construct allows to legitimate the status of the current political actors that are opposed to the cruel and totalitarian former actors. However, the same holds vice versa—exhibition based on the nostalgic narration can legitimize people from the former regime structure if such narration has support among the population.

The trends that might be expected in the nearest future in regard to the interpretation of the socialist past in the successor states would be associated with three competing discourses: "authoritarian," "nostalgic," and "mixed." The last one would attempt to synthesize first two versions by trying to be balanced and critical at the same time. It is important to mention that the appearance of the given trends might be stimulated by each other. Thus, by the appearance of one of them, one might expect to see the mobilization of the community with the ideologically opposite vision resulting in the organization of the exhibition based on the counter-narrative.

Due to the fact that the articulation of personal opinion on the recent past is an important factor of political identification in the contemporary societies of the former Yugoslavia, the topic becomes valuable for serious ideological manipulations. Because of the relative easiness of conversion of the "position" into the political capital, the topic is used for the electoral mobilization of the population. Therefore, the coexistence or coemergence of opposite exhibitions is the result of the struggle that takes place on both the micro level of individuals' everyday life conversations and on the level of political performances. The vision of the communist period plays serious uniting and dividing role and allows to identify the political orientation of the potential voters.

It was shown how the polysemic signs by being put in the different contexts receive a dominant meaning. Thus, such neutral signs as "clothes" or "car" obtain a specific meaning by inclusion into the broader order of other signs or elements. The car is transformed into a symbol of universal prosperity, or segregation; plural styles of clothes—into the symbol of political liberty.

Another important aspect of the analysis is the fields of discursivities that are visible in the analyzed national cases, or, in other words—everything that was left outside the dominant discourse. Thus, what is surprisingly not accumulated in the museum space is such issues as national protests (Croatian and Slovenian Spring), student protests in Kosovo, or labor protests in the industrial zones of Yugoslavia. The cultural life of the 1980s, reach on the emergence of the list of legendary music bands, experimental theater projects together with its important role and influence in the political life of the decade is also predominantly excluded from the museum representation.

Taking into account the tendency of specialization in the research dedicated to Yugoslav life and its dissolution, the emergence of exhibitions that would be focused on the number of specific issues is also very possible. Such approach would allow to focus on the scientific findings and to minimize the possibility of political dominance over the scientific. However, even in such cases, the author (understood as plurality of curators) is never excluded from the political discourse. The exhibition dedicated to the toy production in Yugoslavia that seems to be a cultural or an ethnographic topic with the important function of preserving the heritage and promoting the multicultural environment may become part of the competing discourses and provoke the political public discussions.

According to Luckman and Berger, the rival schools of thought that emerge during the segmentation of the knowledge is the "normal" (keeping in mind the relatives of normality) attempt of defining reality or, in other words, of organizing the hegemonic discourse. Thus, the intention to establish the particular symbolic order and discredit or liquidate the competitive body of knowledge provided by other groups of experts and political actors is the tendency that may be seen as the situation of normal social division. The plurality of thoughts with the possibility to find the public spaces that will represent them has crucial importance for the democratic development of the state and, particularly, because of this, the emergence of the exhibitions dedicated to Yugoslavia with struggling interpretations is the indicator of the social dynamics and of the production of the new meanings.

The dynamism of the collective memory became important characteristics of the analysis of the socialist period of the recent past. And it is extremely important to keep in mind that the role of the Yugoslavia as the narrative construction of the past that is visible in the museums is withal the identification of the state politics for the future of the state. In this perspective, it has a crucial importance for the future study by the various social and political disciplines and should not be neglected and reduced for analysis of the cultural anthropologist or museum study discipline only.

7 DISCUSSIONS

During the last two decades, the interest in the museum studies has dramatically intensified. This is visible through the appearance of the most fundamental research on the history of museums and their role in both nation-states and former colonial empires. The development of the post-colonial theories with the fundamental role of Edward Said, together with the implementation of the Foucadian approach on power relation, and actualization of Gramsi's theory together with neo-Marxists approaches have resulted in some prominent pieces of investigations. Just to mention, Tony Bennet's history of the museum published in 1995, or establishment of the journal *Museum and Society* by the Leicester university, with the first issue launched in 2003.[36] Nevertheless, a museum as the object of research in sociology in general or political sociology in particular is rarely implemented and remains marginalized. Usually, museums are perceived as the field of cultural studies or ethnological research or, as a last resort, the sphere of the historical departments. With the given study, I aimed to analyze museums as the area of research not only in the ethnographic studies but as the object for the sociological, political, and other crosscultural research. Museums viewed as political institutions and the pieces of the complex systems involved in the construction and simultaneous transmission of the national, local, or community vision on the past/present and future might be extremely useful for the further research in political transformations, research on memory studies, migration, globalization, individualization, gender studies, and many other fields. With the overcoming of the underrated potential of museums, the field of sociological studies would enrich its methodological potential while museums may give new challenging findings. The relative easiness to get into the field (their public nature), the relative conciseness, rich visuality, and contextuality of the material provide the research with the broad number of questions to ask and diverse methodologies to get the answers.

[36] Museum and Society journal http://www2.le.ac.uk/departments/museumstudies/museumsociety

In terms of the issue being central to our research—the representation of the socialist period—further investigations might be possible in the directions of further deepening of the data. I have limited my research to the capital cities and by focusing on the history museums. However, the art museums, museums of ethnic minorities, and even museums dedicated to biology or technology could give unexpectedly rich information on the issues such as national and local identity construction, national history and also the cultural patterns, self-imagination and imagination of the Other, the social distance and level of xenophobia, gender prejudice, and many other issues.

For deepening of the given research, it would also be extremely useful to compare the museums located in the capitals with other cities significant for the research. For instance, when talking about Slovenia, one could compare museum located in Ljubljana with two other museums that deal with the recent past: museum in Maribor and in Celje. One of the questions could be the following: what are the reasons to keep the former Yugoslav title as in the case of the Maribor museum, which retained the title The National Liberation Museum.

In the case of Croatia, further studies could be expanded and include not only Zagreb museums but also the place where Broz Tito was born—Kumrovec from one side and the Naked Island from another. It will allow to see more complex picture and compare the competing narratives that possibly exist in two places.

The Serbian case might be enriched by the inclusion of the museums from Vojvodina region. If the focus of the research would include the representation of the 1990s, then Novi Sad may also be included as the towns close to the country's borders. Bosnia and Herzegovina could be further analyzed through the museums representing three main ethnic communities in the country and at the same time compared to the narratives constructed in Serbia. Thus, inclusion of such cities as Banja Luka, Mostar, and Brckowould increase the scientific understanding of the narratives produced and habitualized there.

The production of the narrative of the national victimhood resonate with the conflict in Ukraine, whereby, there is evidence of similarities between

Serbian politics of the 1990s and the current behavior of the Russian government and society in the form of media rhetoric, colonial behavior, and violation of the basic principles of the international law.

Since the annexation of the Crimea and the invasion of the Russian military to the Donbass area, "Bosniazation" or "Balkanization" of Ukraine has become a legitimate formulation that was widespread in Ukrainian media discourses for a while. The main idea, when such statement is applied, is the separation of the country into the enclaves, which led to the fragmentation of the national union into uncontrolled ethnically based parts with the competing, feuding, and scattered memories. "Bosniazation" has become the synonym of the worst scenario for Ukrainian future and is used not only by the journalists but by the analytics as well. Just to mention Oleksandr Sushko (2014), or Taras Voznyak who mentioned the given terms as the possible scenarios of Ukrainian division in their recent publications.[37] Being used in a metaphoric sense, the descriptions usually lack the understanding of the contemporary memory politics in BiH. Therefore, the further comparison of Serbian and Bosnian politics of memory may contribute to the understanding of the chances for the reconciliation for the counties of the "frozen conflict" as well as to analyze the possible scenarios for further development of Ukrainian-Russian geopolitical relations.

In the cases of Kosovo and Macedonia, the inclusion of sites with Albanian (in Macedonia) or a Serbian majority (in Kosovo) or places with mythological connotation for the national history (the case of Kosovo Polje) could help to analyze the complexity of the national narratives and its exclusivist politics. The analysis of the connection between political stakeholders, the policies, and the roles of the directors in this scheme would contribute to the understanding of the position of the museums as the political agents and might throw some light on how to transform the institutions into the places of the transparent and more inclusive nature.

---

[37] Plan Putína—«bosníizatsíya» Ukraini (in Ukrainian), Khvylya. net, September 24, 2014, http://hvylya.net/analytics/politics/plan-putina-bosniyezatsiya-ukrayini.html

8 LIST OF REFERENCES

Adam, Frane, and Matevž Tomšič. 2012. "The Dynamics of Elites and the Type of Capitalism: Slovenian Exceptionalism?" *Historical Social Research* 37 (2): 53–70.

Adeney Thomas, Julia. 2000. "Realizing Memory, Transforming History." In *Museums and Memory*, edited by Susane A. Crane, 93–114. Stanford University Press, pp. 272.

Allcock, John B. 2000. *Explaining Yugoslavia*. New York: Columbia University Press. 499 pp.

Appadurai, Arjun, and Carol Breckenridge. 1991. "Museums are Good to Think: Heritage on View in India." In *Museums and Communities: The Politics of Public Culture*, edited by Ivan Karp, Christine Mullen Kraemer, and Steven D. Lavine, 3455. Washington, DC: Smithsonian Institution Press.

Armatta, Judith. 2010. *Twilight of Impunity: The War Crimes Trial of Slobodan Milosevic*. Duke University Press, pp. 576

Baker, Catherine. 2012. "Prosperity Without Security: the Precarity of Interpreters in Postsocialist, Post-Conflict Bosnia-Herzegovina." *Slavic Review* 71(4): 849–872.

Bal, Mieke. 2008. "Exhibition as Film." In *(Re)visualizing National History: Museology and National Identities in Europe in the New Millennium*, edited by Robin Ostow, 15–46. University of Toronto Press, Scholarly Publishing Division, pp. 256.

Banks, Marcus. 2001. *Visual Methods in Social Research*. Los Angeles, London, New Dehli: Sage Publications, pp. 208.

Barrett, Jennifer. 2011. *Museums and the Public Sphere*. Chichester: Wiley-Blackwell, pp. 208.

Barrett, Michelle. 1991. *The Politics of Truth. From Marx to Foucault*. Cambridge: Polity Press, pp. 208.

Bartlett, Djurdja. 2010. "Žuži Jelinek: The Incredible Adventures of a Socialist Chanel." In *Remembering Utopia: The Culture of Everyday Life in Socialist Yugoslavia*, edited by Breda Luthar and Marusa Pusnik, 407-427. Washington, DC: New Academia Publishing, pp. 468.

Bartlett, William. 2003. *Croatia: Between Europe and the Balkans*. Routledge, pp. 196.

Basha, Rozafa. 2007. *Proposal for Adaptation of the Emin Gjiku Stable Building in Prishtina*. http://www.hdm.lth.se/fileadmin/hdm/alumni/papers/CMHB_2007/Kosova__Rozafa_Basha_Emin_Gjiku_stable_paper.pdf.

Bebler, Anton. 2002. "Slovenia's Smooth Transition." *Journal of Democracy* 13 (1): 127–40.

Bencard, Adam. 2014. "Presence in the Museum: On Metonymies, Discontinuity and History Without Stories." *Museum & Society* 12 (1): 29-43.

Bennett, Tony, Mike Savage, Elizabeth Bortolaia Silva, Alan Warde, Modesto Gayo-Cal, and David Wright, eds. 2008. *Culture, Class, Distinction*. Taylor & Francis, pp. 336.

Bennett, Tony. 1995. *The Birth of the Museum: History, Theory, Politics*. London & New York: Routledge, pp. 288.

Berger, Peter L., and Thomas Luckmann. 1991. *The Social Construction of Reality: A Treatise in the Sociology of Knowledge*. Penguin Books, pp. 256

Bieber, Florian. 2003. "Montenegrin Politics Since the Disintegration of Yugoslavia." In *Montenegro in Transition. Problems of Identity and Statehood*, edited by Florian Bieber, 11–42. Baden-Baden: Nomos.

Bieber, Florian. 2014. "Introduction." In *Debating the end of Yugoslavia*, edited by Florian Bieber, Armina Galijaš, and Rory Archer. Centre for Southeast European Studies, University of Graz, Farnham and Burlington: Ashgate, pp. 276.

Bleich, Erik. 2011. *The Freedom to be Racist?: How the United States and Europe Struggle to Preserve Freedom and Combat Racism*. New York: Oxford University Press, pp. 224.

Boghossian, Paul A. 2001, February 23. *What is Social Construction?* New York University. http://as.nyu.edu/docs/IO/1153/socialconstruction.pdf

Bošković, Aleksandar. 2013. "Yugonostalgia and Yugoslav Cultural Memory: Lexicon of Yu Mythology." *Slavic Review* 72 (1): 54–78.

Boyer, Dominic. 2010. "From Algos to Autonomos: Nostalgic Eastern Europe as Postimperial Mania." In *Post- Communist Nostalgia*, edited by Maria Todorova and Zsuzsa Gille, 17–28. New York and Oxford: Berghahn Books, pp. 310.

Boym, Svetlana. 2001. *The Future of Nostalgia*. New York: Basic Books, pp. 432.

Buric, Fedja. 2010. "Dwelling on the Ruins of Socialist Yugoslavia: Being Bosnian by Remembering Tito." In *Post- Communist Nostalgia*, edited by Maria Todorova and Zsuzsa Gille, 227–243. New York and Oxford: Berghahn Books, pp. 310.

Burr, Vivien. 1995. *An Introduction to Social Constructionism*. London: Sage, pp. 208.

Burr, Vivien. 2003. *Social Constructionism*. London and New York: Routledge, pp. 229.

Cabada, Ladislav. 2008. "Decentralization Processes in Croatia and Slovenia." *Politics in Central Europe* 4 (1): 24–37.

Chilton, Paul. 2005. "Missing Links in Mainstream CDA: Modules, Blends and the Critical Instinct." In *A New Agenda in (Critical) Discourse Analysis: Theory, Methodology and Interdisciplinarity*, edited by Ruth Wodak and Paul Chilton, 19–52. Amsterdam and Philadelphia: John Benjamins Publishing Company, pp. 321.

Christensen, Carleton B. 2008. *Self and World—From Analytic Philosophy to Phenomenology*. Berlin and New York: Walter de Gruyter, pp. 378.

Clegg, S.R., M. Kornberger, and T. Pitsis. 2005. *Managing and Organization: An Introduction to Theory and Practice*. London: Sage, pp. 712.

Cooke, Paul. 2005. *Representing East Germany Since Unification: From Colonization to Nostalgia*. Oxford and New York: Berg, pp. 256.

Cox, John K. 2005. *Slovenia: Evolving Loyalties*. London and New York: Routledge, pp. 228.

Crampton, R.J. 2002. *Eastern Europe in the Twentieth Century—And After*. London and New York: Routledge, pp. 526.

Crane, Susane A., ed. 2000. *Museums and Memory*. Stanford University Press, pp. 272.

Crooke, Elisabeth. 2008. "Putting Contested History on Display: The Uses of the Past in Northern Island." In *(Re)visualizing National History: Museology and National Identities in Europe in the New Millennium*, edited by Robin Ostow, 90–107. University of Toronto Press, Scholarly Publishing Division, pp. 256.

Cvijic, Srdjan. 2008. "Swinging the Pendulum: World War II History, Politics, National Identity and Difficulties of Reconciliation in Croatia and Serbia." *Nationalities Papers: The Journal of Nationalism and Ethnicity* 36 (4): 713–40.

Dames, Nicholas. 2001. *Amnesiac Selves: Nostalgia and Forgetting, and British Fiction, 1810–1870.* Oxford: Oxford University Press, pp. 312.

Damijan, P. Joze. 2004. "Reentering the Market of the Former Yugoslavia." In *Slovenia. From Yugoslavia to the European Union*, edited by Mojmir Mrak, Matija Rojec, Carlos Silva-Jauregui, 334–49. Washington, DC: The World Bank.

David, Matthew, and Carole D. Sutton. 2011. *Social Research: An Introduction.* Sage Publications, pp. 680.

DiMaggio, Paul J. and Walter W. Powell. 1983. "The Iron Cage Revisited: Institutional Isomorphism and Collective Rationality in Organizational Fields." *American Sociological Review* 48(2): 147-160.

Dimova, Rozita. 2012. "The Ohrid Festival and Political Performativity in the Contemporary Republic of Macedonia." *Journal of Balkan and Near Eastern Studies* 14 (2): 229–244.

Djurić, Dubravka, and Miško Suvaković, eds. 2003. *Impossible Histories. Historical Avant-gardes, Neo-avant-gardes, Post-avant-gardes in Yugoslavia, 1918–1991.* Cambridge: The MIT Press, pp. 520.

Drake Wilson, Diana. 2000. "Realizing Memory, Transforming History." In *Museums and Memory*, edited by Susane A. Crane, 115–36. Stanford University Press, pp. 272.

Dulić, Dragana. 2011. "Serbia after Milošević: The Rebirth of a Nation." In *Civic and uncivic values: Serbia the post-Milošević era*, edited by Ola Listhaug, Sabrina P. Ramet, and Dragana Dulić, 20–47. Budapest and New York: Central European University Press, pp. 468.

Duncan, Carol, and Alan Wallach. 2004. "The Universal Survey Museum." In *Museum Studies. An Anthology of Contexts*, edited by Bettina Messias Carbonell, 46–61. Malden, MA: Blackwell, pp. 680.

Dzankic, Jelena. 2013. "Montenegro and the EU: Changing Contexts, Changins Roles." In *Europe and the Post-Yugoslav Space*, edited by Branislav Radeljic, 109–131. Ashgate, pp. 244.

Elder-Vass, Dave. 2010. *The Causal Power of Social Structures: Emergence, Structure and Agency.* Cambridge University Press, pp. 234.

Elsie, Robert. 2012. *A Biographical Dictionary of Albanian History.* New York: I.B. Tauris, pp. 480.

Ernst, Wolfgang. 2000. "Archi(ve)textures of Museology." In *Museums and Memory*, edited by Susane A. Crane, 17–34. Stanford University Press, pp. 272.

Fairclough, Norman. 2004. *Analysing Discourse.* London and New York: Routledge.

Fairclough, Norman. 2005. "Critical Discourse Analysis in Transdisciplinary Research." In *A New Agenda in (Critical) Discourse Analysis: Theory, Methodology and Interdisciplinarity*, edited by Ruth Wodak and Paul Chilton, 53–70. Amsterdam and Philadelphia: John Benjamins Publishing Company.

Fehr, Michael. 2000. "A Museum and its Memory: the Art of Recovering History." In *Museums and Memory*, edited by Susane A. Crane. Stanford University Press, pp. 272.

Felberg, Tatjana Radanović, and Ljiljana Šarić. 2013. "Discursive Construction of Language Identity through Disputes in Croatian and Montenegrin Media." *Scando-Slavica* 59 (1): 7–31.

Feldmann, Magnus. 2006. "Emerging Varieties of Capitalism in Transition Countries: Industrial Relations and Wage Bargaining in Estonia and Slovenia." *Comparative Political Studies* 39 (7): 829–54.

Fisher, Sharon. 2006. *Political change in post-Communist Slovakia and Croatia: From Nationalist to Europeanist.* Palgrave Macmillan.

Flere, Sergej. 2014. "The Dissolution of Yugoslavia as Reflected Upon by Post-Yugoslav Sociologists." In *Debating the end of Yugoslavia,* edited by Florian Bieber, Armina Galijaš, and Rory Archer, 81–96. Centre for Southeast European studies, University of Graz, Farnham and Burlington: Ashgate, pp. 276.

Flick, Uwe. 2011. *An Introduction to Qualitative Research,* 4th ed. Sage, pp. 616.

Gee, James Paul. 2011. *An Introduction to Discourse Analysis: Theory and Method,* 3rd ed. Routledge, Abingdon and New York: pp. 248.

Gergen, Kenneth J. 1998. "Constructionist Dialogues and the Vicissitudes of the Political." In *The Politics of Constructionism,* edited by I. Velody. London, Thousand Oaks, New Dehli: Sage, pp. 256.

Gergen, Kenneth J. 2009. *An Invitation to Social Construction.* Second Edition, Sage, pp. 200.

Graan, Andrew. 2013. "Counterfeiting the Nation?: Skopje 2014 and the Politics of Nation Branding in Macedonia." *Cultural Anthropology* 28(1): 161-179.

Grandits, Hannes. 2008. "Dynamics of Socialist Nation-Building: The Short Lived Programme of Promoting a Yugoslav National Identity and Some Comparative Perspectives." *Two Homelands* 27. http://twohomelands.zrc-sazu.si/onlinejournal/DD_TH_27.pdf.

Guha-Thakurta, Tapati. 2004. *Monuments, Objects, Histories: Institutions of Art in Colonial and Postcolonial India.* Columbia University Press, pp. 432.

Hajdarpasic, Edin. 2008. "Museums, Multiculturalism, and the Remaking of Postwar Sarajevo." In *(Re)Visualizing National History: Museums and National Identities in Europe in the New Millennium,* edited by Robert Ostow, 109–38. University of Toronto Press, pp. 256.

Harper, Douglas. 1998. "An Argument for Visual Sociology." In *Image-based Research,* edited by Jon Prosser, 20–35. London: Routledge, pp. 328.

Hill, Duncan, ed. 2012. *Kronika Vojne od leta 1914 do danes* [Chronics of War 1914 to the Present Day]. Jezero: Morfem, pp. 322.

Hinchman, Lewis P. and Sandra K. Hinchman. 1997. *Memory, Identity, Community: The Idea of Narrative in the Human Sciences.* State University of New York Press. Hupchick, Dennis P. 2002. *The Balkans: From Constantinople to Communism.* New York and Basingstoke: Palgrave, pp. 468.

Huyssen, Andreas. 1995. *Twilight Memories: Marking Time in a Culture of Amnesia.* New York and London: Routledge, pp. 302.

Janev, Goran. 2010. "Narrating the Nation, Narrating the City." Cultural Analysis 10 (2011): 3-21.

Jenne, Erin K., and Florian Bieber. 2014. "Situational Nationalism: Nation-building in the Balkans, Subversive Institutions and the Montenegrin Paradox." *Ethnopolitics: Formerly Global Review of Ethnopolitics* 13 (5): 431–60.

Jewitt, Carey, and Rumiko Oyama. 2008. "Visual Meaning: a Social Semiotic." In *Handbook of Visual Analysis,* 134–56. Los Angeles, London, New Delhi, and Singapore: Sage, pp. 224.

Jorgensen, Marianne, and Louise Phillips. 2002. *Discourse Analysis as Theory and Method.* London, Thousand Oaks, and New Delhi: SAGE Publications, pp. 230.

Jović, Dejan. 2004. "'Official Memories' in Post-authoritarianism: An Analytical Framework." *Journal of Southern Europe and the Balkans* 6 (2): 97–108.

Judah, Tim. 2009. "Yugoslavia is Dead: Long Live the Yugosphere Good News From the Western Balkans." In *Papers on South Eastern Europe*. Issue 1, edited by Spyros Economides and Ivan Kovanović. London, UK: LSEE—Research on South Eastern Europe.

Kavanagh, Gaynor. 1996. "Making Histories, Making Memories." In *Making Histories in Museums*, edited by Gaynor Kavanagh, 1–14. London and New York: Leicester University Press, pp. 285.

Kemp, Wolfgang. 1991. "Visual Narratives, Memory and the Medieval Esprit du Systéme." In *Images of Memory: On Remembering and Representation*, edited by Susanne Küchler and Walter Melion, 87–108. Washington, DC and London: Smithsonian Institution Press, pp. 256.

Kienzler, Hanna. 2010. "*The Differential Impact of War and Trauma on Kosovar Albanian Women Living in Post-War Kosova*." A thesis submitted to McGill University, McGill University, Montreal.

Knoblauch, Hubert, Alejandro Baer, Eric Laurier, Sabine Petschke, and Bernt Schnettler. 2008. "Visual Analysis. New Developments in the Interpretative Analysis of Video and Photography." *Forum Qualitative Sozialforschung/Forum: Qualitative Social Research* 9 (3).

Kostadinova, Tonka. June 10–17, 2011. "Conference paper 'A Three Piece Puzzle': The Relationship between Culture, International Relations and Globalization." In: *Cultural Diplomacy in War-Affected Societies: International and Local Policies in the Post-Conflict (re) Construction of Religious Heritage in Former Yugoslavia*. Institute for Cultural Diplomacy, Berlin Academy for Cultural Diplomacy.

Kovačević, Filip. 2014. "Montenegro's Political System." *Academic Foresights* 10 (January–April). http://www.academic-foresights.com/Montenegro.pdf.

Kuljic, Todor. 2010. *Umkampfte Vergangenheiten. Die Kultur der Erinnerung im postjugoslawischen Raum*. Berlin: Verbrecher Verlag, pp. 220.

Kurin, Richard. 1991. "Cultural Conservation through Representation: Festival of India Folklife Exhibitions at the Smithsonian Institution." In *Exhibiting Cultures: The Poetics and Politics of Museum Display, Exhibiting Cultures: The Poetics and Politics of Museum Display*, edited by Ivan Karp and Stephen D. Levine. Washington, DC: Smithsonian Institution Press, pp. 480.

Laclau, Ernesto, and Chantal Mouffe. 1985. *Hegemony and Socialist Strategy. Towards a Radical Democratic Politics*. London: Verso, pp. 208.

Lafazanovski, Ermis. 2006. "Skopje: Nostalgic Places and Utopian Spaces." *Etnologica Balkanica* 10: 63–75.

Lampe, John R. 1996. *Yugoslavia as History: Twice There was a Country*. Cambridge University Press, pp. 512.

Latour, Bruno. 2013. *An Inquiry Into Modes of Existence: An Anthropology of the Moderns*. Translated by Catherine Porter. Cambridge: Harvard University Press, pp. 520.

Leeuwen, Van Theo. 2008. *Discourse and Practice: New Tools for Critical Discourse Analysis*. Oxford University Press, pp. 129.

Liddiard, Mark. 1996. “Making Histories of Sexuality.” In *Making Histories, Making Memories*, edited by Gaynor Kavanagh, 163–75. London and New York: Leicester University Press, pp. 285.

Lock, Andy, and Tom Strong. 2010. *Social Constructionism: Sources and Stirrings in Theory and Practice*. Cambridge, New York, Melburne: Cambridge University Press, pp. 402.

Lozic, Vanja. 2011. “National Museums in Bosnia-Herzegovina and Slovenia: A Story of Making ‘Us’.” In *Building National Museums in Europe 1750–2010*, edited by Peter Aronsson and Gabriella Elgenius, 69–96. Conference proceedings from EuNaMus, European National Museums: Identity Politics, the Uses of the Past and the European Citizen, Bologna 28–30 April 2011. EuNaMus Report No 1. Linköping University Electronic Press. http://www.ep.liu.se/ecp_home/index.en.aspx?issue=064.

Luke, Timothy W. 2002. *Museum Politics: Power Plays at the Exhibition*. Minneapolis and London: University of Minnesota Press, pp. 296.

Luthar, Breda, and Marusa Pusnik, eds. 2010. *Remembering Utopia: The Culture of Everyday Life in Socialist Yugoslavia*. Washington, DC: New Academia Publishing, pp. 468.

Luthar, Oto, ed. 2013. *The Land Between: A History of Slovenia*. Frankfurt am Main, Berlin, Bern, Bruxelles, New York, Oxford,Wien: Peter Lang International Academic Publishers, pp. 562.

Makarovič, Matej, and Matevž Tomšič. 2010. “Democrats, Authoritarians and Nostalgics: Slovenian Attitudes Toward Democracy.” In *Contemporary World between Freedom and Security*, edited by Alenka Pandiloska Jurak and Uroš Pinterič, 461–87. Ljubljana: Vega, pp. 517.

Makaš, Emily Gunzburger. 2012. “Museums and the History and Identity of Sarajevo.” Conference paper presented at: *European Association for the Urban History, 11th International Conference on Urban History Cities*, August 29 –September 1, 2012, Prague, Czech Republic, 1–13.

Malcolm, Noel. 1996. *Bosnia: A Short History*. Pepermac, 384. pp.

Malcolm, Noel. 1998. *Kosovo: A Short History*. New York: University Pres New York, pp. 492.

Martin, John, and Ruth Martin. 2004. “History Through the Lens: Every Picture Tells a Story.” In *Seeing is Believing? Approaches to Visual Research*, edited by Christopher J. Pole, 9–22. University of Leicester, UK, Amsterdam, Boston, Heidelberg, London, New York, Oxford Paris, San Diego, San Francisco, Singapore, Sydney, and Tokyo: Elsevier.

Matonin, Yevgeny. 2012. *Jozip Broz Tito*. Moscow: The Young Guard. (in Russian) (Матонин, Евгенийю 2012. Иосип Броз Тито, Москва: Молодая гвардия), pp. 480.

Mattioli, Fabio. 2014. “Regimes of Aesthetics: Competing Performances Surrounding the Skopje 2014 Plan.” *In Mirroring Europe Ideas of Europe and Europeanization in Balkan Societies*, edited by Tanja Petrović, 64-88. Koninklijke and Leiden: Brill Publishing, pp. 224.

Mazzucchelli, Francesco. 2012. “What Remains of Yugoslavia? From the Geopolitical Space of Yugoslavia to the Virtual Space of the Web Yugosphere.” *Social Science Information* 51 (December): 631–48.

Mehmeti, Leandrit I. 2013. “Democratization in Kosovo: The Role of International Institutions.” In *Europe and the Post-Yugoslav Space*, edited by Branislav Radeljic, 183–209. Ashgate, pp. 244.

Merriman, Nick, and Nima Poovaya-Smith. 1996. "Making Culturally Diverse Histories." In *Making Histories, Making Memories*, edited by Gaynor Kavanagh, 176–87. London and New York: Leicester University Press, pp. 285.

Meyer, John W. and Brian Rowan. 1977. "Institutionalized Organizations: Formal Structure as Myth and Ceremony." *American Journal of Sociology* 83: 340–363.

Miheljak, Vlado, and Niko Toš. 2005. "The Slovenian Way to Democracy and Sovereignty." In *Political Faces of Slovenia: Political Orientations and Values at the End of the Century*, edited by Niko Toš and Karl H. Muller, 23–48. Wien: Edition Echoraum, pp. 551.

Moll, Nicolas. 2014. "Fragmented memories in a fragmented country: memory competition and political identity-building in today's Bosnia and Herzegovina." *Nationalities Papers* 41 (6): 910-935.

Morrison, Kenneth. 2009. *Montenegro: A Modern History*. London and New York: IB Tauris, pp. 264.

Norkus, Zenonas. 2012. *On Baltic Slovenia and Adriatic Lithuania: A Qualitative Comparative Analysis of Patterns in Post-Communist Transitions*. Budapest and New York: Central European University Press, pp. 375.

Olick, Jeffrey K. 1999. "Collective Memory: The Two Cultures." *Sociological Theory* 17 (3): 333–48.

Olick, Jeffrey K., and Joyce Robbins. 1998. "Social Memory Studies: From 'Collective Memory' to the Historical Sociology of Mnemonic Practices." *Annual Review of Sociology* 24: 105–40.

Ostow, Robin. 2008. "Introduction: Museums and National Identities in Europe in the Twenty-First Century." In *(Re) Visualizing National History: Museums and National Identities in Europe in the New Millennium*, edited by R. Ostow. University of Toronto Press, pp. 256.

Paltridge, Brian. 2008. *Discourse Analysis: An Introduction*. London, New Delhi, New York, Sydney: Continuum, pp. 296.

Panofsky, Erwin. 1970. *Meaning in the Visual Arts*. Harmondsworth and Middlesex: Penguin Books, pp. 464.

Pappas, Takis S. 2005. "Shared Culture, Individual Strategy and Collective Action: Explaining Slobodan Milošević's Charismatic Rise to Power." *Southeast European and Black Sea Studies* 5 (2): 191–211.

Perritt, Henry H. 2010. *The Road to Independence for Kosovo: A Chronicle of the Ahtisaari Plan*. New York: Cambridge University Press, pp. 328.

Phillips, John. 2004. *Macedonia: Warlords and Rebels in the Balkans*. Yale University Press, pp. 240.

Plate, Liedeke, and Anneke Smelik, eds. 2013. *Performing Memory in Art and Popular Culture*. New York and London: Taylor & Francis, pp. 230.

Popović, Helena. 2014. "Croatia." In: *MEDIA Integrity Matters: Reclaiming Public Service Values in Media and Journalism*, edited by Brankica Petković, 193–257. Ljubljana: Peace Institute, Institute for Contemporary Social and Political Studies, pp. 446.

Radstone, Susannah. 2007. *The Sexual Politics of Time: Confession, Nostalgia, Memory*. Abingdon and New York: Routledge, pp .264.

Ramet, Sabrina P. 2002. *Balkan Babel: The Disintegration Of Yugoslavia From The Death of Tito To The Fall Of Milosevic*, 4th ed. Westview Press, pp. 448.

Ramet, Sabrina P. 2005. *Thinking about Yugoslavia Scholarly Debates about the Yugoslav Breakup and the Wars in Bosnia and Kosovo.* Cambridge, New York, Melbourne: Cambridge University Press, pp. 348.

Ramet, Sabrina P. 2006. *The Three Yugoslavias: State-Building and Legitimation, 1918–2005.* Indiana University Press, pp. 784.

Ramet, Sabrina P. 2007. "The Dissolution of Yugoslavia: Competing Narratives of Resentment and Blame." *Sudosteuropa* 55 (1): 26–69.

Ramet, Sabrina P. 2010. "Politics in Croatia since 1990." In *Central and Southeast European Politics since 1989*, edited by Sabrina P. Ramet, 258–85. Cambridge: Cambridge University Press, pp. 600.

Ramet, Sabrina P. 2011. "Serbia's Corrupt Path to the Rule of Law: An Introduction." In *Civic and uncivic values: Serbia the post-Milošević era*, edited by Ola Listhaug, Sabrina P. Ramet, and Dragana Dulić, 1–19. Budapest and New York: Central European University Press, pp. 468.

Reed, Michael. 2005. "Reflections on the 'realist turn' in Organization and Management Studies." *Journal of Management Studies* 42: 1621–44.

Rev, Istvan. 2008. "The Terror of the House." In *(Re)visualizing National History: Museology and National Identities in Europe in the New Millennium*, edited by Robin Ostow, 47–89. University of Toronto Press, Scholarly Publishing Division, pp. 256.

Richardson, John. 2007. *Analysing Newspapers: An approach from Critical Discourse Analysis.* Basingstoke and New York: Palgrave Macmillan, pp. 280.

Riedlmayer, András. 2000. "Museums in Kosovo: A First Postwar Assessment." *Bosnia Report.* UK: Bosnian Institute. http://www.bosnia.org.uk/bosrep/marjune00/museums.cfm.

Rigney, Ann. 2012. "Reconciliation and Remembering: (how) does it work?" *Memory Studies, 5*: 209-226.

Ritzer, George. 2010. *Sociological Theories*, 8th ed. McGraw-Hill Higher Education.

Rose, Gillian. 2001. *Visual Methodologies: An Introduction to the Interpretation of Visual Materials.* London, Thousand Oaks, and New Delhi: SAGE Publications, pp. 229.

Rossos, Andrew. 2008. *Macedonia and the Macedonians: A History.* Hoover Institution Press, pp. 392.

Roudometof, Victor. 2002. *Collective Memory, National Identity, and Ethnic Conflict: Greece, Bulgaria, and the Macedonian Question.* Westport: Praeger, pp. 280.

Runia, Eelco. 2006. "Presence." *History and Theory* 45: 1–29.

Schuman, Michael. 2004. *Croatia.* Facts on File, pp. 128.

Schutz, Alfred, and Thoman Luckmann. 1973. *The Structures of the Life-World,* Vol. 1. Northwestern University Press, pp. 335.

Shrum, W. and Ricardo B. Duque. 2008. "Film and Video in Qualitative Research." In *The Sage Encyclopedia of Qualitative Research Methods*, edited by Lisa M. Given, 348–50. New York, London, New Delhi, and Singapore: SAGE, pp. 1072.

Slovenska Kronika 20. Stoletja 1941–1995. 1995. Ljubljana: Nova revija, pp. 457.

Stojanović, Dubravka. 2011. "Value Changes in the Interpretations of History in Serbia." In *Civic and uncivic values: Serbia the post-Milošević era*, edited by Ola Listhaug, Sabrina P. Ramet, and Dragana Dulić, 221–41. Budapest and New York: Central European University Press, pp. 468.

Sushko, Oleksandr. 2014. *After the Ukraine-Russia War: Is There a Sustainable Solution?* PONARS, Eurasia Policy Memo, No. 356.

Swain, G. and N. Swain. 2009. *Eastern Europe since 1945.* Basingstoke: Palgrave Macmilla.

Sztompka, Piotr. 2007. *Visual Sociology: Photography as Method of Research.* Moscow: Logo (in Russian) (Штомпка, Петр. Визуальная социология. Фотография как метод исследования.—Москва: Логос).

Tantrigoda, Pavitra. 2013. "The Limits of the Visual in the "War Without Witness"." *Sociology of the Visual Sphere.* Edited by Regev Nathansohn and Dennis Zuev. 12–24.New York: Routledge, pp. 192.

Terrell, John. 1991. "Disneyland: The Future of Museum Anthropology." *American Anthropologist* 93 (1): 149–51.

Tomsic, Matevž, and Lea Prijon. 2013. "Elites, Ideologies and Crisis in Slovenia." *Raziskave in Razprave 6 (2): 71–116.*

Unkovski-Korica, Vladimir. 2014. "Workers' Councils in the Service of the Market: New Archival Evidence on the Origins of Self-Management in Yugoslavia 1948–1950." *Europe-Asia Studies* 66 (1): 108–34.

Van Leeuwen, Theo. 2008. "Semiotics and Lconography." In *Handbook of Visual Analysis,* edited by Carey Jewit Theo van Leeuwen, 92–118. Los Angeles, London, New Dehli, and Singapure: Sage.

Vankovska, Biljana. 2013. "Constitutional Engineering and Institution-Building in the Republic of Macedonia (1991-2011)." In *Civic and Uncivic Values in Macedonia: Value Transformation, Education and Media,* edited by Sabrina P. Ramet, Ola Listhaug and Albert Simkus, 87-108. Palgrave Macmillan, pp. 347.

Velikonja, Mitja. 2008. *Titostalgia A Study of Nostalgia for Josip Broz.* Ljubljana: Peace Institute, pp. 132.

Velikonja, Mitja. 2013. "Between Collective Memory and Political Action: Yugonostalgia in Bosnia-Herzegovina." In *Bosnia-Herzegovina since Dayton: Civic and uncivic values,* edited by Ola Listhaug, and Sabrina P. Ramet, 351–68. Ravenna : Longo Editore, pp. 426.

Vladisavljević, Nebojša. 2014. "Does Scholarly Literature on the Breakup of Yugoslavia Travel Well?" In *Debating the end of Yugoslavia,* edited by Florian Bieber, Armina Galijaš, and Rory Archer, 67–80. Centre for Southeast European studies, University of Graz, Farnham and Burlington: Ashgate, pp. 276.

Volčič, Zala. 2007. "Yugo-Nostalgia: Cultural Memory and Media in the Former Yugoslavia." *Critical Studies in Media Communication* 24 (1): 21–38.

Vučetić, Radina. 2010. "Džubox (Jukebox)—The First Rock-n-roll Magazine in Socialist Yugoslavia." In *Rememebering Utopia: The Culture of Everyday Life in Socialist Yugoslavia,* edited by Breda Luthar and Marusa Pusnik, 145–64. New Academia Publishing, pp. 468.

Vuletic, Dean. 2010. "European Sounds, Yugoslav Visions: Performing Yugoslavia at the Eurovision Song Contest." In *Rememebering Utopia: The Culture of Everyday Life in Socialist Yugoslavia,* edited by Breda Luthar and Marusa Pusnik, 121–44. New Academia Publishing, pp. 468.

Wilkening, Susie, and James Chung. 2009. *Life strategies of the Museums Visitors. Building Engagement Over a Lifetime.* The AAM Press, pp. 67.

Williams, Paul. 2007. *Memorial Museums: The Global Rush to Commemorate Atrocities*. Bloomsbury Academic, pp. 224.

Wortel, Elise, and Anneke Smelik, 2013. "Textures of Time: A Becoming-Memory of History in Costume Film." In *Performing Memory in Art and Popular Culture*, edited by Liedeke Plate and Anneke Smelik, 185–200. New York and London: Taylor & Francis, pp. 230

Zambelli, Nataša. 2010. "A Journey Westward: A Poststructuralist Analysis of Croatia's Identity and the Problem of Cooperation with the International Criminal Tribunal for the former Yugoslavia." *Europe-Asia Studies* 62 (10): 1661–82.

Zubkovych, Alina. 2014. "Reactivating the Past: Case Study Analysis of the Non-museum-based Yugo-nostalgic Exhibition in Serbia." *Research and Discussion* 8, (1): 99–129.

Zubkovych, Alina. 2015a. "Transformation of the Public Space Perception: Case Study of the Museum of Yugoslav History." In *Multi-faced Social Transformations: Challenges and Studies*, edited by Elena Danilova, Matej Makarovic, and Alina Zubkovych, 157–80. *Cambridge Scholars Publishing*, pp. 245.

Zubkovych, Alina. 2015b. "Interpreting the Past: The Competing Memories of the Yugoslavian Period Through the Case Study Analysis of Slovenian History Museum and Private Exhibition." *Innovative Issues and Approaches in Social Sciences* 8 (1): 109–28.

***ibidem*.eu**